Mary Wentworth Newman

Poetry of the Pacific

Selections and Original Poems from the Poets of the Pacific

Mary Wentworth Newman

Poetry of the Pacific
Selections and Original Poems from the Poets of the Pacific

ISBN/EAN: 9783337005016

Printed in Europe, USA, Canada, Australia, Japan

Cover: Foto ©Thomas Meinert / pixelio.de

More available books at **www.hansebooks.com**

POETRY OF THE PACIFIC:

SELECTIONS AND ORIGINAL POEMS

FROM THE

POETS OF THE PACIFIC STATES.

EDITED BY

MAY WENTWORTH.

———•◆•———

SAN FRANCISCO:

PACIFIC PUBLISHING COMPANY,

305 MONTGOMERY STREET.

1867.

MANUFACTURED BY
CASE, LOCKWOOD & CO.,
Printers and Bookbinders,
HARTFORD, CONN.

ELECTROTYPED BY
LOCKWOOD & MANDEVILLE,
HARTFORD, CONN.

PREFACE.

IN presenting this volume, but little need be said, except that the compiler has earnestly endeavored to make it as complete as possible, and to render it a pleasant book for reference in after years, as belonging to the early days of literature in California.

It must be remembered that California is still an infant state, a Hercules in the cradle.

The toiling gold seekers have had but little time or encouragement to cultivate *belle lettres*, and to the future we look to develop the rich mines of intellect, as well as those of gold and silver.

One or two writers, whose names are familiar to the public, are not represented, their poems having been omitted in deference to their wishes. Others may have been overlooked, but in no case through intentional neglect. The compilation of this volume has been attended with much care and difficulty, and it is to be hoped that enough of beauty and merit may be found in its pages, to commend it to the acceptance of a generous public.

MAY WENTWORTH.

CONTENTS.

CONTENTS.

CONTENTS.

viii   CONTENTS.

POETRY OF THE PACIFIC.

OLIVIA.

BY EDWARD POLLOCK.

WHAT are the long waves singing, so mourn-
    fully, evermore?
What are they singing so mournfully, as they
    weep on the sandy shore?
"Olivia, oh, Olivia!"—what else can it seem
    to be!
"Olivia, lost Olivia, will never return to thee!"
"Olivia, lost Olivia"—what else can the sad
    song be?
—"Weep and mourn, she will not return, she
    can not return to thee!"

And strange it is, when the low wind sighs,
    and strange, when the loud winds blow,
In the rustle of trees, in the roar of the storm,
    in the sleepiest streamlet's flow,

Forever, from ocean or river, ariseth the same
    sad moan
—"She sleeps, let her sleep, wake her not—it
    were best she should rest—and alone.
Forever the same sad requiem comes up from
    the sorrowful sea,
For the lovely, the lost Olivia, who can not
    return to me!

Alas! I fear 'tis not in the air, or the sea or the
    trees, that strain,
I fear 'tis a wrung heart-aching, and the throb
    of a tortured brain,
And the shivering whisper of startled leaves,
    and the sob of the waves as they roll;
I fear they are only the echo of the song of a
    suffering soul—
Are only the passionless echo of the voice that
    is ever with me,
—"The lovely, the lost Olivia, will never re-
    turn to thee!"

I stand in the dim grey morning, where once
    I stood, to mark
Gliding away along the bay like a bird, her
    white wing'd bark;

And when, through the Golden Gate, the sun-
    set radiance rolled,
And the tall masts melted to thinnest shreds
    in the glowing haze of gold,
I said, "to thine arms I give her, oh kind and
    shining sea,
And in one long moon from this June eve,
    you shall let her return to me."

But the wind from the far spice islands came
    back and it sang with a sigh—
"The ocean is rich with the treasure it has hid-
    den from you and the sky.
And where, amid rocks and the green sea-weed
    the storm and the tide were at war,
The nightly-sought waste was still vacant, when
    I looked to the cloud and the star;
And soon the sad wind and dark ocean unceas-
    ingly sang unto me,
"The lovely, the lost Olivia, will never return
    to thee!"

Dim and still the landscape lies, but shadowless
    as heaven;
For the growing morn, and the low-west moon
    on everything shine even:

The ghosts of the lost have departed, that
    nothing can ever redeem;
And Nature, in light, sweet slumber, is dream-
    ing her morning dream.
'Tis morn, and our Lord has awakened, and
    the souls of the blessed are free.
Oh come from the caves of the ocean—Olivia
    return unto me.

What thrills me?—what comes near me? Do
    I stand on the sward alone?
Was that a light wind or a whisper?—a touch,
    or the pulse of a tone?
Olivia! whose spells from thy slumber, my
    broken heart sway and control,
At length bringest thou death to me, dearest
    —or rest to my suffering soul?
No sound but the psalm of the ocean—
    "Bow down to the solemn decree—
"The lovely, the lost Olivia, will never re-
    turn to thee!"

And still are the long waves singing, so
    mournfully evermore;
Still are they singing so mournfully, as they
    weep on the sandy shore—

"Olivia—lostOlivia!"—so ever 'tis doomed
    to be—

"Olivia—lost Olivia—will never return to
    thee."

"Olivia, lost Olivia"—what else could the
    sad song be?—

'"Weep and mourn, she will not return—she
    can not return to thee."

THE CHANDOS PICTURE.

The bell far off beats midnight; in the dark
    The sounds have lost their way and wan-
        der slowly;
Through the dead air, beside me, things cry
    "hark!"
And whisper words unholy.

A hand, as soft as velvet, taps my cheek,
    These gusts are from the wings of unseen
        vampires ;
How the thick dust on that last tome doth
    speak
    Its themes, dead kings and empires :

This is the chamber, ruined, waste, forlorn ;
    Shred of its old-time guilding, paint and
        splendor;
And is there none its dim decay to mourn,
    In mystic strains and tender ?

Why waits no harper gray, with elfin hand,
    In tuneless chords to harshly hail the
        stranger
Who treads the brink of an enchanted strand,
    In mist and midnight danger?

I watch and am not weary; all night long
 The stars look shimmering thro' the yawn-
 ing casement,
And the low ring of their unvarying song
 I hear without amazement.

How the hours pass! with that low murmur
 blent,
 That is a part of time, yet thrills us only
When all beside is silent, and close pent,
 The heart is chilled and lonely.

I watch, and am not weary; I have heard
 Light steps and whispers pass me, all un-
 daunted;
Have seen pale spectres glide where nothing
 stirred,
 Because the place is haunted.

And wherefore watch I fearless? Wherefore
 come
 These things with windy garments, hover-
 ing round me?
Whence are the tongues, the tones, the stifled
 hum,
 That welcomed, and have bound me?

Lo! on the wall, in mist and gloom high
    reared,
  A luminous face adorns the structure hoary;
Light-bearded, hazel-eyed, and auburn-haired,
  And bright with a strange glory.

'Tis but the semblance of a long dead one,
  A light that shines and is not; clouds are
    o'er it;
Yet in the realm of thought it beams a sun,
  And stars grow pale before it.

There tend the tones; thro' that wan atmos-
    phere
  Glide the faint spectres with a stately mo-
    tion,
Slowly, as cloudy ships to sunset steer,
  Along the airy ocean.

Shades of the great but unremembered dead,
  Moan there, and moaning, ever restless
    wander;
For in the presence of that pictured head,
  Their waning shapes grow grander.

And here watch I, beneath those eyes sublime,
  A listening to the soft, resounding numbers,
That float like wind along the waves of time,
  And cheat me of my slumbers.

And who shall calm the restless sprites that
    rove
  In the mute presence of that painted poet?
In their vain triumph of old wars or love,
  No future times shall know it.

For, "oh!" they cry, "his song has named
    us not!
  He stretched no hand to lift the pall flung
    o'er us."
And still they moan and shriek—"Forgot,
    forgot!"
  In faint and shivering chorus.

Mightiest of all, my master, dare not I
  Touch the shrunk chords thy hand divine
    hath shaken ;
How would the heroes of the days gone by
  Throng round me, and awaken!

Oh! many a heart the worthiest—many a
     heart
  Cold now, but once an angel's warm, bright
     dwelling,
Waits but the minstrel's wizard hand, to
     start
  With life immortal swelling!

And thou, so missed—where art thou?   On
     what sphere
  Of nightless glory hast thou built thine
     altar?
What shining hosts bow down thy song to
     hear,
  Thy heart the harp and psalter?

Thy dust is mingled with thy native sod;
  Exhaled like dew, thy soul, that ranged
     unbounded;
And who shall dare to tread where Shakspeare
     trod,
  Or strike the harp he sounded!

ADALINE.

THERE were two lovers long ago
　　—Ah, well-a-day!
Of spirits warm, but chaste as snow,
　　That things so pure should pass away!
And oft alone and whispering lowly,
Among the woods they wandered slowly,
When twilight shades were sweet and holy;
　　　　For clearest shine
　　　　Love glances, then, like thine,
　　　　My tender, bright-eyed Adaline!
And this true lover and the maiden,
　　In ages vanished, lost and gone,
Made for themselves a dim star-aiden,
　　All in the silent dawn.

Oft in the moon's transparent mist,
　　—Ah, well-a-day'
Before the sun the clouds had kist,
　　That things so kind should fade away!
They met while stars above were shining,
Where leaves and flowers were intervining,
Her head upon his breast reclining;

As often thine
Reposes upon mine,
My fair, my peerless Adaline!
And thus the lover and the maiden
In ages vanished, lost and gone,
Dwelt fearless in their dim star-aiden,
All in the silent dawn.

He saw no beauty, she no truth,
—Ah, well-a-day!
Save in her form and his fresh youth—
That things so fond should pass away!
And sooth to say she looked serenely,
Among the wet leaves glancing greenly,
With her fair head reclined and queenly;
Tho' not like thine,
Not with thy grace divine,
My own beloved Adaline!
So the fond lover and the maiden,
In ages vanished, lost and gone,
Stood dreaming in their dim star-aiden,
All in the silent dawn.

They loved and they were blest; they died,
   —Ah, well-a-day!
The bridegroom and his fair young bride,
   That things so bright should fade away!
The flowers are wet, the stars are gleaming,
They sleep while all around is beaming,
Not even of each other dreaming;
      Close—closer twine
      Thy soft white arms in mine—
      Oh, could I save thee, Adaline!
Oh love—oh death! alas the maiden
   And the lover, in the ages gone,
Passed from their pleasant dim star-aiden,
   Like shadows from the dawn.

A LEGEND OF THE PACIFIC COAST.

SOUTHWARD of our gates of gold
An hundred leagues, as the tale is told,
There lieth, a mile below the sea,
A city that was, and yet shall be;
Drowned for its sins, but yet to rise
As shriven souls ascend the skies.

I have been through that city in a dream;
Where its turrets through the blue waves
        gleam
I have stood, when the moon to the rippled
        wave
The ghastly ghost of sunlight gave;
Through the avenues long, accursed by crime,
In the shadows of the olden time,
In a vision I wandered, and walked amid
The streets where numberless things lie hid
That nameless seemed, and strange to me,
In those sunless solitudes down in the sea.

The hand of Time, that spectre grim,
Has never reached down through the water
        · dim;

But pillar and column are standing there
Erect as they stood above in the air;
And, save that o'er all the slimy water
   A cold and glittering film hath cast—
As northern winds, unpitying, scatter
   Ice on the trees as they hurry past—
The mirror-like marbles untarnished shine
As when first they went down in the sparkling
     brine.

The waving sea-weeds, rank and tall,
Like ivy, are clinging to tower and wall,
And the glittering dolphin and ravenous
   shark
Are gliding around in the chambers dark.
There the arms of the polypus are seen
Like a spider's mesh in the water green,
And a thousand wonderful creatures sleep
Motionless, silently down in the deep.

There sitteth a form on a marble throne,
   The form of a maiden young and fair;
But the water hath turned the body to stone,
   And hardened the curls of her raven hair;
Yet her full dark eyes are open, and seem
Forever to flash with a lambent beam;

But her rounded arms and bosom white,
Have a deathly cast in that sadden'd light.

When the loving waves of a thousand years
    Shall have washed from those walls of guilt
        the stain—
As sin is washed out by the penitent's tears,
    That city will start from her slumbers
        again;
And surely 'twill be strange to mark
Each tower as it leaves its chambers dark—
Springing up into life, unbound and free,
From those sunless solitudes down in the
    sea.

WHEN THE SOLEMN MIDNIGHT
LONELY.

When the solemn midnight lonely
    Sleeps around me deep and still,
And the gentle night-breeze only
    Murmurs music on the hill;
When the seal of noiseless slumber
    Closes every eye but mine,
And illusions without number
    Visions for the dreamer twine;
Then, sweet maiden, still beside me
    I thy gentle image see,
As though lingering to guide me
    From my wandering to thee.

When the ruddy morn leaps shining
    From the oriental wave,
And the laughing hours are twining
    Flow'rs to deck each other's grave;
When the fragrant blossoms lure me
    O'er the green and dewy lawn,
And her purple banners o'er me
    Waves the rosy-handed dawn;

2

Still, sweet maiden, still beside me,
   I thy gentle image see,
As though lingering to guide me
   From my wandering to thee.

O that future hours some token
   To my spirit would supply!
That the spell should ne'er be broken,
   That thy charm should never die.
Gladly would I hail the morrow
   That should bid me rove no more;
Seeking still through life to borrow
   Sweets from time's illusive store;
Then, sweet maiden, still beside me
   Thy dear image would I see,
Sighing, seeking still to guide me
   Back from wandering to thee.

SONG.

Ye stars that look at me to-night,
How beautiful you seem!
For I have found my spirit's light,
The seraph of my dream.
Oh! never half so bright before
Have I beheld you shine,
For heaven itself looks lovelier,
To lover's eyes like mine!

Alas! I fear when midnight waits
To catch my voice, in vain
The listeners at your golden gates
Will hear some other twain,
Whose hearts like ours, in melody,
Will sadly throb and sigh,
To see how calmly you behold
E'en lovers kiss, and—die!

EVENING.

THE air is chill and the day grows late,
And the clouds come in through the Golden
Gate:
Phantom fleets, they seem to me,
From a shoreless and unsounded sea;
Their shadowy spars, and misty sails,
Unshattered, have weathered a thousand gales:
Slow wheeling, lo! in squadrons gray,
They part, and hasten along the bay;
Each to its anchorage finding way.
Where the hills of Saucelito swell
Many in gloom may shelter well;
And others—behold—unchallenged pass
By the silent guns of Alcatras:
No greetings, of thunder and flame, exchange
The armed isle and the cruisers strange.
Their meteor flags, so widely blown,
Were blazoned in a land unknown;
So, charmed from war, or wind, or tide,
Along the quiet wave they glide.

What bear these ships?—what news, what
    freight
Do they bring us through the Golden Gate?
Sad echoes to words in gladness spoken,
And withered hopes to the poor heart-bro-
    ken:
Oh, how many a venture, we
Have rashly sent to the shoreless sea;
How many an hour have you and I,
Sweet friend, in sadness seen go by,
While our eager, longing thoughts were ro-
    ving,
Over the waste, for something loving,
Something rich, and chaste, and kind,
To brighten and bless a lonely mind;
And only waited to behold
Ambition's gems, affection's gold,
Return, as "remorse," and "a broken vow,"
In such ships of mist as I see now.

The air is chill and the day grows late,
And the clouds come in through the Golden
    Gate,
Freighted with sorrow, heavy with woe;—
But these shapes that cluster, dark and low,
To-morrow shall be all aglow!

In the blaze of the coming morn these mists,
Whose weight my heart in vain resists,
Will brighten and shine and soar to heaven,
In thin white robes, like souls forgiven;
For heaven is kind, and everything,
As well as a winter, has a spring.
So, praise to God! who brings the day,
That shines our regrets and fears away;
For the blessed morn I can watch and wait,
While the clouds come in through the Gold-
        en Gate.

'TIS AUTUMN, MARY.

BY LYMAN GOODMAN.

When April's tears had melted down
   Into the bosom of the earth,
And woke the snow-drop on the hill,
   And gave the yellow crocus birth,
I came, dear Mary, half afraid,
   And sat me down close by your side;
We talked of love, and then I asked
   If you would be my darling bride.
You dropped your head a moment then,
   Then laid your little hand in mine,
And looked into my eyes, and said,
   When Autumn comes, I will be thine.

The meadows whitened, and the hills
   Seemed bursting into golden speech,
The apple-blossoms filled the air,
   And rosy wreaths hung on the peach;
And thick among the purple blooms
   The birds were flitting all the day—
The linnet swung upon the bough,
   And poured a merry roundelay;

The robbin trimmed his crimson breast,
    And watched his love among the leaves,
The swallow skimmed along the lea,
    Or clung beneath the shelving eaves.

And June was all a perfect glow,
    So fraught with melody and bloom
My soul disrobed itself and bathed
    In seas of music and perfume.
And all your being seemed to drink
    The love and beauty round us shed—
Your eyes were filled with tender light,
    And love were all the words you said;
And day by day you grew more fair,
    And day by day I loved you more,
And longer, Mary, than at first
    I lingered at your vine-hung door.

The summer ended all too soon;
    Too soon the chilling night-winds came
And breathed upon the beauteous earth,
    And changed the forest into flame.
The little birds grew sad and mute,
    And left us for their sunny home,
The flowers only smiled and said,
    We now must sleep till Spring shall come

Yes, Mary, everything I loved
   Seemed going from me, and my heart
Grew into tears as one by one
   I saw the beautiful depart.

And now 'tis Autumn, and again
   I come and sit me by your side,
And think of all the words you said
   When first I asked you for my bride;
And how my life grew into light,
   And how the sunlight turned to wine,
When in the golden Autumn-days
   You promised that you would be mine.
Not mine?   Dear Mary, in my breast
   The flowers of love no more shall bloom;
And I will leave my heart to rest
   Beside you, Mary, in the tomb.

2*

IDEALINE.

BY LYMAN GOODMAN.

As though by magic means, I drew
   The vail of Fairy-land aside,
   And saw the gorgeous pageants glide
In misty forms before my view;
So sweet a vision floats between
Me and the world!   A fairy mien,
So airy, beautiful and light,
   I scarcely dare to lisp a prayer,
Lest it should vanish from my sight,
   And like the rainbow melt in air,
Leaving my soul like the weeping sky,
Where shadows still on its bosom lie.

Pygmalion, were thy powers mine,
   And thy sweet aid, O Queen of Love!
  I might the fair ideal prove,
And mould the delicate outline
Of that bright eidolon of life,
And call the conscious beauty—wife.
O sweeter than a seraph's tongue
   Could syllable, to see each grace,
Each tender elegance of form,
   Each soft expression take its place;

Till from their combination were grown
A faultless symmetry—and my own!

And yet I trust, O love of God!
  Somewhere in this wide world of ours,
  Among its gardens of wild flowers,
In some sweet spot I have not trod,
'Mid melody, and light, and bloom,
Ambrosial airs and rich perfume,
Where silver-sounding fountains ring
  Their wedding-bells upon the wind,
Drest in the bridal-wreath of Spring,—
  I fondly hope, and trust to find,
In maidenhood's own form divine,
My beautiful IDEALINE.

THE FAIR TAMBOURINIST.

BY LYMAN GOODMAN.

WITH feet half-naked and bare,
  And dress all tattered and torn—
With a penny here and a mockery there,
  And floods of derision and scorn—
She wanders the street wherever her feet
  Weary and willing are borne,
With an eye as bright and a cheek as fair
  As the earliest blush of morn.

Wandering up and down
  And driven from door to door,
A jest for every idle clown
  And a butt for every boor:
While the velvet-slippered, in satin and lace,
  Go rustling by her side,
With a frozen heart and curtained face,
  And a lip up-curled with pride.

So beautiful, yet so frail;
  So willing, and yet so weak:—
O what if the heart should fail,
  And a heavenly purpose break,

And the dens and kennels and brothels of
  Hell
Another poor victim should hold—
A celestial spark be quenched in the dark,
  And an angel bartered for gold!

No wonder the heart should fail,
  And a heavenly purpose fade—
The eye grow dim and the cheek grow pale—
  Where none stand ready to aid;
No wonder the lairs and cradles of Hell
  So many poor victims should hold,
When the good are content to worship their
  God,
  And the rich to worship their gold!

Move patiently on, O Earth,
  Till Mercy's wandering dove
Shall fly to the realm of its birth
  And rest in the bosom of love!
Move patiently on till the crucified Christ
  Shall gather His radiant crown
From the lowly flowers and bleeding hearts
  Which the world has trampled down!

MINNIE ADAIR.

BY LYMAN GOODMAN.

O I thought her so pretty, and called her my
    own,
    As the rich sunlight played in and out of
      her curls,
As her little white feet 'mid the violets shone,
    And her clear laughter rippled through ru-
      bies and pearls.
        Through June's golden mazes
        Of pansies and daisies
We wandered and warbled our songs on the
    air;
        O the birds, a whole tree full,
        Were never more gleeful
Than I and my sweet little Minnie Adair!

They come now and tell me that you're to
    be wed,
    That rank has encircled your brow with its
      rays,
But when in your beautiful palace you tread,
    With many to flatter you, many to praise,

Shall June's golden mazes
Of pansies and daisies,
And the bare-footed playmate who thought
you so fair—
Who wept at your sadness,
And shared in your gladness—
Be lost in their splendor, O Minnie Adair!

THE NIGHT-WATCH.

BY LYMAN GOODMAN.

Hark!
How hoarse through the sedges the river
doth flow,·
And the wind snarls and mutters, unwilling
to blow;
The clock in the belfry strikes solemn and
slow—
Hark!
Weird, phantom-like voices are whispering
low,
Here in the dark!

Strange!
And a feeling creeps over me, chilling, un-
known—
Not a feeling of dread, though I start at each
tone,
As I sit here and listen in darkness alone.
Strange!
And the hand that mine touches is colder
than stone—
Wonderful change!

Dead?

I know the lips answer me not when I speak,

And the pulses are silent, and icy the cheek;

Yet it seems but a spell which affection can
break—

Dead?

Why, I gave her the bridal-ring only last
week—

Next, to be wed!

Hush!

Through the casement the moonlight creeps
stealthily in—

How softly it sleeps on her white marble
chin!

Lo! it steals to her lips, now so pallid and
thin—

Hush!

Like a spirit it touches the lily-leaf skin
With a rose flush!

Vain!

The organ is broken, the melody flown

To swell the grand anthems in temples unknown;

No art can restore the lost beauty and tone—
    Vain!
Yet I'll kiss the mute lips, for they still are
    my own—
        All that remain!

        Rest!
The gray dawn is breaking, the night-watch
    is done;
But the long night of sorrow is only begun—
No morning to gladden, no life-cheering sun;
        Rest!
And dream in thy slumber, sweet angel, of
    one
        Loving unblest!

GERALDINE.

BY RINGGOLD.

A SIESTA.

It happened, shall I e'er forget?
　One day that my young bride—
My own, my charming Geraldine,
　Sat sewing by my side.

The afternoon so lovely was,
　A walk with her I planned;
So having laid her needle by,
　We went forth hand in hand.

And wand'ring thro' the grand old woods,
　No words my joy could tell,
I thought within my soul, I ne'er
　Had loved her half so well.

At length we reached a dark retreat,
　Within the wood that slept,
Where often in our courting day,
　The trysting we had kept.

A fascinating, fearfully
  Romantic spot was this,
Upon the very edges of
  A dizzy precipice.

And old fantastic oaks, their arms
  Far o'er the brink did throw,
While a thread of limpid water leaped
  Into the gulf below.

And thus we stood—I gazing with
  Delight upon my dove,
For beauty is so precious in
  The being that we love.

When suddenly a step she took,
  I scarce had time to think ;
She stooped to pluck a flower that grew
  Upon the fatal brink.

Transfixed I stood—I could not speak,
  Nor warning could bestow ;
Alas! I saw her balance lost,
  She headlong fell below.

I shrieked—I sprang to save her,
  When wide awake I saw,
My nose, the laughing Geraldine,
  Was tickling with a straw.

SAN PABLO.

BY RINGGOLD.

Oh! it is a night of beauty, that hath drawn
     me thus away
From the glare of lighted chambers, with
     their gallant guests and gay;
With a tenderness she greets me, for the wind
     is sweet and low,
And like thoughts that move a quiet heart,
     its pulses come and go.

See! the moon upon her cloud-car rides, of
     pure and pearly gray,
Scatt'ring fragments of a shattered world of
     silver o'er the bay,
And beyond the hills that fade away as dis-
     tance swims between,
There the tall sierra through the misty deep
     is dimly seen.
Like a line of lurid lava grows the night-fire
     on the strand,
While in creamy folds the white smoke lifts
     itself above the land,

Till upon the breeze it rises to a region still
    and clear,
Hanging like a wide and motionless pavilion
    in the air.

Oh! it is a night of beauty, for the stars
    shine sweetly down,
With a quiet gaze, as loving eyes have looked
    into our own;
'Tis a night to charm the spirit with the touch
    of other years,
Where embalmed lie youth's precious joys,
    or youth's most precious tears.

With a gentle hand adown the silent past she
    guideth me,
As I move among the forms of things that
    have ceased to be;
And with sure, unerring footstep leadeth to
    a scene of bliss,
Folded in the quiet shadows of a night the
    twin to this.

I am standing by the wicket of a cottage,
    while the moon
Throws her waste of liquid silver over all
    the leafy June;

And with happy smile a maiden's young and
    joyous face is seen,
Peeping through the shaded loopholes of the
    ivy's glittering green.

From that home where sped her happy youth
    in blest security,
With the perfect trust of innocence she com-
    eth forth to me;
Then with half-directed footsteps we go wan-
    d'ring through the shade
Of an aisle of pointed arches by the lofty
    cedars made.

And I'm telling her a tale of love in earnest
    words, and low
As the laugh of dimpled waters on their jour-
    ney as they go;
And she listens without chiding me, nor bids
    me to depart,
But comes trembling like a frightened bird,
    and nestles near my heart.

But alas! I dream; the picture fast and faster
    fades away,
And I wake amid the solitude that wraps the
    lonely bay;

And my heart will not be comforted, but
  keep its store of love
For the golden land that lieth there—those
  starry heights above.

3

SPIRIT OF LOVE.

BY T. H. UNDERWOOD.

THE bright stars no longer are gleaming,
    And slowly arises the mist;
The sun o'er the hill-tops is beaming,
    And the lips of the lilies are kissed;
The dew-drops all sparklingly tremble,
    On the leaflets that gracefully bend—
Such beauty no art may resemble,
    As Nature to Morning can lend.

The rapturous zephyrs are teeming
    With perfume of fresh blooming flowers,
Even Youth, in its passionate dreaming,
    Hath nothing so bright in its bowers,—
For Cupid with me has been playing,
    Though my heart he may never deceive,
For such things as he has been saying
    No lover would dare to believe.

The rosebuds are opening and blushing,
    While nectar the humming-bird sips—
Thy cheek the same rose-hue is flushing,
    And tempting as nectar thy lips.

One rose in its sweet passion sighing,
    Now gives me a delicate hint;
Thy beauty—its splendor out-vieing,
    Lends dreaming a rosier tint.

A spirit of love seems pervading
    The heart of the least living thing,
Nor is the sweet passion degrading,
    Love ruleth from peasant to king.
Though fresh-tinted roses are faded,
    By glow of thy beauty so bright,
Yet a *Queen* is never degraded
    By the love of her humblest knight.

COMING REST.*

BY T. H. UNDERWOOD.

I've walked the variegated slope
   That rises like a floral screen,
   Festooned deceitfully between
The "Valley" and the Land of Hope.

No more upon the hill I wait
   To see the curtains hanging high,
   Looped up against a golden sky,
Athwart the Morning's crystal gate.

No more beneath its jeweled arch
   The bright beatitudes of youth,
   Undoubting Love, sweet Hope and
     Truth,
Like angels of the morning, march.

---

* This poem was written only a few days before the death of the author.

Now, on the Western slope I go,
　　With weary step and brimming eyes,
　　The "Valley and the Shadow" rise,
The "River" is not far below.

I hear the voices in the Vale
　　Of falling sands along the shore,
　　The same that I have heard before
Far-off and fitful on the gale.

And now I feel the treacherous land
　　Beneath my trembling pathway stirred,
　　And nearer still the dash is heard,
And closer steals the crumbling sand.

The hollow sounds beneath my way
　　Reveal a grave at every tread,
　　They come like welcomes of the dead:
Amen! mute brothers of the clay.

Amen! I neither smile nor weep,
　　But calmly listen while the shore
　　With never-ceasing break and roar
Is dropping in the waters deep.

The most I know, or seek to know,
   Is that this aching heart will rest
   In peace upon the Mother-breast,
Shut from a weary world of woe.

TO A WAVE.

BY COL. BAKER.

Dost thou seek a star, with thy swelling crest,
Oh! wave that leaves thy mother's breast?
Dost thou leap from the prisoned depths
 below
In scorn of their calm and constant flow?
Or art thou seeking some distant land,
To die in murmurs upon the strand?

Hast thou tales to tell of the pearl-lit deep,
Where the wave-whelmed mariner rocks in
 sleep?
Canst thou speak of navies that sunk in pride,
Ere the roll of their thunder in echo died?
What trophies, what banners, are floating free
In the shadowy depths of that silent sea?

It were vain to ask, as thou rollest afar,
Of banner, or mariner, ship or star;
It were vain to seek in thy stormy face
Some tale of the sorrowful past to trace.
Thou art swelling high, thou art flashing free,
How vain are the questions we ask of thee!

I, too, am a wave on a stormy sea;
I, too, am a wanderer, driven like thee;
I, too, am seeking a distant land
To be lost and gone ere I reach the strand.
For the land I seek is a waveless shore,
And they who once reach it shall wander no
      more.

RELICS OF THE OLD HOMESTEAD.

BY G. T. SPROAT.

THERE stand the two old elm-trees,
　That grew before the door,
In which the birds are singing,
　Their sunny song of yore.

And o'er the shaded pathway,
　The rows of lilacs meet,
And the long rank grass is waving,
　Where trod the children's feet.

And troops of singing swallows,
　Are circling overhead,
Above where stood the homestead,
　With its low walls, brown and red.

The babbling brook in the orchard,
　Still sings the same old song,
As it dances and leaps in the sunshine,
　O'er the step-stones all day long.

3*

And the well-curb worn and mossy,
    And the water-trough by its side,
And the pool where the geese came at morn-
        ing,
    And the cattle at even-tide.

The spot where we children sported,
    And sent our ships to sea,
Richer far than old Castilian merchants,
    With their home-bound argosy.

And the place where the bees lived in sum-
        mer,
    And in the soft June hours,
Came laden with honied treasures,
    From the rifled garden flowers.

And the sheepcot in the meadow,
    And the spot by the green hill's side,
Where the lambs used to frolic and gambol,
    From morning to eventide.

These, these now, are all that is left me,
    On the green earth's sunny side,
Of the spot where my mother loved me—
    The home where my father died.

THE LIGHT AT THE WINDOW.

BY DENNAR STEWART.

THERE's a battered, shattered, tumble-down
    house,
  Just over across the street,
With every clapboard so loose that a mouse
  Could knock them off with his feet.
'Tis low and small, and dingy and brown,
  And never knew whitewash or paint;
Its thriftless garden, with fences down,
  Of negligence maketh complaint.
And yet 'tis not utterly drear and lorn,
For in noontime bright, or roseate morn,
A visitor glad, of the sunbeam born,
  Enters in at the little window.

I watched to-night, as the darkness fell,
  That house like a spectre lone—
Its bleak, gaunt frame, in the shadowy spell
  Unto frightful likeness grown.
The wild winds growl, and night comes apace,
  With storm-clouds gathering on high;
The house looms up, with its haggard face
  Threat'ning the weird-like, angry sky:

When lo! to a love-cot its walls transform,
For sweetly smiling through blackness and
      storm,
Cheerfully glowing, and ruddily warm,
   Shines a light from the little window.

And many tenements human, I ween,
   May be found in every street,
Squalidly wretched, and abjectly mean,
   Whom no man careth to greet;
Sin-stained, woe-bestamped, vilest of vile,
   Yet not by their God forsaken,
For a beating heart is theirs the while,
   A casement where light is taken.
It may be a dust-covered spider's lair,
And Demon with Angel may wrestle there;
Yet with brotherly deed and loving prayer,
   Let your light shine in at the window.

Give as the Sun gives—like him persevere,
   With a boon for every day;
For a time will come, be it far or near,
   That heralds the answering ray.
Some Sorrow's night, or Temptation's storm,
   Shall be gilded with its beaming.
The hut a heavenly mansion form,

Each pane with radiance streaming.
You may be sleeping the long, dreamless
    sleep,
For still one sows where another will reap;
Yet when you're crossing the Death-river
    deep,
    There will be a light in the window!

THE BURIED HEART.

BY DENNAR STEWART.

"I sleep, but my heart waketh."

TREAD lightly, love, when over my head,
　　Beneath the daisies lying,
And tenderly press the grassy bed
　　Where the fallen rose lies dying.

Dreamless I sleep in the quiet ground,
　　Save when, your foot-fall hearing,
My heart awakes to the old-loved sound
　　And beats to the step that's nearing.

Bright shone the moon, last eve, when you
　　　came—
　　Still dust for dust hath feeling—
The willow-roots whispered low the name
　　Of him who weeps while kneeling.

The lily-cup holds the falling tears,
　　The tears you shed above me;
And I know through all these silent years
　　There's some one still to love me.

Oh, softly sigh; for I hear the sound
   And grieve me o'er your sorrow;
But leave a kiss in the myrtle mound—
   I'll give it back to-morrow.

Whisper me, love, as in moments fled,
   While I dream your hand mine taketh;
For the stone speaks false that says "She's
     dead;"
"I sleep, but my heart awaketh."

THE ENROBING OF LIBERTY.

BY CAXTON.

THE war-drum was silent, the cannons were
    mute,
  The sword in its scabbard lay still,
And Battle had gathered the last autumn
    fruit
  That crimson-dyed river and rill;
When a goddess came down from her man-
    sion on high,
  To gladden the world with her smile,
Leaving only her robes in the realm of the
    sky,
  That their sheen might no mortal beguile.

As she lit on the earth she was welcomed by
    Peace—
  Twin-sisters in Eden of yore,
But parted forever, when fetter-bound Greece
  Drove her, exiled and chained, from her
    shore.
Never since had the Angel of Liberty trod,
  In virginal beauty below,

.

But chased from the earth, she had mounted
    to God,
  Despoiled of her raiment of snow.

Our sires gathered round her, entranced with
    her smile;
  Rememb'ring the foot prints of old
She had graven on grottoes, in Scio's sweet
    Isle,
  Ere the doom of fair Athens was told.
"I am naked," she cried! "I am homeless
    on earth,
  Kings, princes, and lords, are my foes,
But I stand undismayed though an orphan
    from birth,
  And condemned to the region of snows!"

"Hail! Liberty, hail!"—our fathers ex-
    claim,—
  "To the glorious land of the West,
With a diadem bright, we will honor thy
    name,
  And enthrone thee America's Guest!
We will found a great nation, and call it thine
    own,
  And erect here an altar to thee,

Where millions shall kneel at the foot of thy
    throne,
    And swear, to forever BE FREE!"

Then each brought a vestment her form to
    enrobe,
    And screen her fair face from the sun,
And thus she stood forth as the Queen of
    the globe,
    When the work of our fathers was done.

A circlet of stars round her temples they
    wove,
    That gleamed like Orion's bright band;
And an emblem of power, the Eagle of Jove,
    They perched like a bolt in her hand:
On her forehead a scroll that contained but a
    line,
    Was written in letters of light,
That our great CONSTITUTION forever might
    shine
    A sun to illumine the night?

Her feet were encased in broad sandles of
    gold,
    That riches might spring in her train;

Whilst a warrior's casque, with the visor up-
    rolld,
  Protected her tresses, and brain.
Round her waist, a bright girdle of satin was
    bound,
  Formed of colors so blended, and true,
That when as a banner, the scarf was un-
    wound,
  It floated the RED, WHITE and BLUE!

Then Liberty calm, leant on Washington's
    arm,
  And spoke in prophetical strain:
"Columbia's proud hills I will shelter from
    ills,
  Whilst her mountains and oceans remain.
But palsied the hand, that would pillage the
    band
  Of sisterhood stars in my crown,
And death to the knave, whose sword would
    enslave
  By striking your great Charter down!"

Your Eagle shall soar, this Western world
    o'er,
  And carry the sound of my name,

Till monarchs shall quake, and its confines
    forsake,
  If true to your ancestral fame!
Your banner shall gleam like the polar star's
    beam,
  To guide through Rebellion's Red Sea,
And on battle 'twill wave, both to conquer
    and save,
  If borne by the hands of the free!

LABOR.

BY FRANK SOULE.

Despise not labor! God did not despise
The handicraft which wrought this gorgeous
  globe,
That crowned its glories with yon jeweled
  skies,
And clad the earth in nature's queenly robe.
He dug the first canal—the river's bed,
Built the first fountain in the gushing spring,
Wove the first carpet for man's haughty tread,
The warp and woof of his first covering.
He made the pictures painters imitate,
The statuary's first grand model made,
Taught human intellect to recreate,
And human ingenuity its trade.
Ere great Daguerre had harnessed up the sun,
Apprenticeship at his new art to serve,
A greater artist greater things had done,
The wondrous pictures of the optic nerve.
There is no deed of honest labor born,
That is not Godlike; in the toiling limbs
Howe'er the lazy scoff, the brainless scorn,
God labored first; toil likens us to him.

Ashamed of work ! mechanic, with thy tools,
The tree thy axe cut from its native sod,
And turns to useful things—go tell to fools,
Was fashioned in the factory of God. .
Go build your ships, go build your lofty dome,
Your granite temple, that through time en-
　　　dures,
Your humble cot, or that proud pile of
　　　Rome,
His arm has toiled there in advance of yours.
He made the flowers your learned florists scan,
And crystalized the atoms of each gem,
Ennobled labor in great nature's plan,
And made it virtue's brightest diadem.
Whatever thing is worthy to be had,
Is worthy of the toil by which 'tis won,
Just as the grain by which the field is clad
Pays back the warming labor of the sun.
'Tis not profession that ennobles men,
'Tis not the calling that can e'er degrade,
The trowel is as worthy as the pen,
The pen more mighty than the hero's blade.
The merchant, with his ledger and his wares,
The lawyer with his cases and his books,
The toiling farmer, with his wheat and tares,
The poet by the shaded streams and nooks,

The *man*, whate'er his work, wherever done,
If intellect and honor guide his hand,
Is peer to him who greatest state has won,
And rich as any Rothschild of the land.
All mere distinctions based upon pretense,
Are merely laughing themes for manly hearts,
The miner's cradle claims from men of sense
More honor than the youngling Bonaparte's.
Let fops and fools the sons of toil deride,
On false pretensions brainless dunces live;
Let carpet heroes strut with parlor pride,
Supreme in all that indolence can give,
But be not like them, and pray envy not
These fancy tom-tit burlesques of mankind,
The witless snobs in idleness who rot,
Hermaphrodite 'twixt vanity and mind.
Oh son of toil, be proud, look up, arise,
And disregard opinion's hollow test,
A false society's decrees despise,
He is most worthy who has labored best.
The sceptre is less royal than the hoe,
The sword, beneath whose rule whole nations
      writhe,
And curse the wearer, while they fear the
      blow,
Is far less noble than the plough and scythe.

There's more true honor on one tan-browned
    hand,
Rough with the honest work of busy men,
Than all the soft-skinned punies of the land,
The nice, white-kiddery of upper ten.
Blow bright the forge—the sturdy anvil ring,
It sings the anthem of king labor's courts,
And sweeter sounds the clattering hammers
    bring,
Than half a thousand thumped piano-fortes.
Fair are the ribbons from the rabbet-plane,
As those which grace my lady's hat or cape,
Nor does the joiner's honor blush or wane
Beside the lawyer, with his brief and tape.
Pride thee, mechanic, on thine honest trade,
'Tis nobler than the snob's much vaunted
    pelf.
Man's soulless pride his test of worth has
    made,
But thine is based on that of God himself.

WATCHING BESIDE HIM.

BY FRANK SOULE.

THE leaves turn yellow on the mournful
    willow,
  November's waves are sighing on the shore;
And there's a fading cheek upon the pillow,
    That shall feel health no more.
The leaves are falling, and my friend is dy-
    ing,
  Comes the destroyer nearer day by day,
And like the leaves on Autumn's breezes
    flying,
    His poor life flits away.
But now the foliage and his life were vernal,
  How soon their Spring and Summer glow
    hath fled!
I would have had their beauty made eternal—
    Ah me! but dust instead!

The leaves have fallen! on the Autumn ed-
    dies,
  The last pale spectres float and disappear,
And one poor body—there his quiet bed is—
    Is all that's left me here.

4

All that is left me of his manly powers,
   All that is left of life so good and brief,
All faded like the first frost-bitten flowers,
   And Autumn's withered leaf.
In night's dark hours his spirit spread her
     pinions,
   Left in our clinging arms alone his form,
Heaven lighted through the dark's obscure
     dominions,
   The starless gloom and storm.

While by his faded form, so sad and lonely,
   I sit, O mighty Monarch, I implore:
Tell me, is life but this, this tell me only
   This and no more?
A few fair hopes, that never can be real,
   A few joys passing like the fleeting breath?
Is immortality but an ideal
   That terminates with death?
Of all I loved so much, so dearly treasured,
   His manly beauty and his comely grace,
By this dear faded form may life be measured,
   And this pale, silent face?

There comes no answer, though my heart is
    crying,
  No message from the spirit gone before,
I hear, instead, the yeasty waves replying
    In sobs upon the shore.
I hear the night-winds in the branches toning,
  Or rustling with the sere and fallen leaf,
Their sad responses to my inward moaning,
    In pity to my grief.
And so in loneliness, and doubt, and sorrow,
  I listen to each night hour's lagging tread,
And silent wait the coming of to-morrow,
    In watch beside the dead.

BURIED AND BORN.

BY FRANK SOULE.

LAST night, with faces turned toward the
    west,
  We stood beside a sepulchre sublime,
And saw an old friend passing to his rest,
  Beside his fathers in the tomb of Time;
Amid the darkness and the splashing rain,
  Our dear companion's shadowy form was
    laid,
No more to bear the crime, and sin, and pain,
  The weary record of his life had made;
And through the shadows flickering and dim,
Saw myriad spectres beautiful, or grim.

A thousand phantoms! deeds without a name,
  Faults, failings, vices, taking shape and
    form,
Out from the past year's garnered harvest
    came,
  Accusing gnomes afloat upon the storm.
Whatever ills the dying year had known,
  Like evil spirits hovered o'er the scene,

The deathless seeds by human passion sown,
  Sprung to full harvest. Yet with brows
    serene
Each good deed in an angel form drew near,
And smiled approval o'er the dying year.

We laid him down to rest with grateful tears,
  Each virtue praised, and every fault for-
    given,
Beside his kindred of the buried years,
  Alone with Night, Eternity, and Heaven.
Twelve struck the clock. Dear silent friend
    adieu!
  And turning—what's this vision fresh and
    fair,
As turns to roseate tints the orient blue,
  Flings out from fading night her golden
    hair?
A virgin form, a rising queen appears,
Crowned with the glories of ancestral years.

Oh, bright-eyed beauty of the glowing morn,
  Oh, red-lipped ruler of the new-made day,
Fair goddess of our destinies unborn,
  While round thy pearly brow the first
    beams play,

Hear this our prayer: Turn from our land
    the wrath
  Of deep-offended Heaven, and through
    the land
Wide spread the flowers of Peace through
    every path,
  And scatter blessings with a liberal hand;
And ere thy queenly tread o'er earth be done,
Unite our jarring elements as one.

So from the buried past our hearts shall turn,
  Made wiser by the lessons it hath taught,
New wisdom from the passing present learn,
 . To do the deeds that answer to the thought;
So from the furnace of the years agone,
  The white heat where our constancy was
    tried,
Our souls shall issue with full harness on
  In strength and manhood, proved and pu-
    rified;
So with our banner for the rignt unfurled,
  To dare and bear and battle for the world.

I FEEL I'M GROWING AULD, GUDE-WIFE.

BY JAMES LINEN.

I feel I'm growing auld, gude-wife—
 I feel I'm growing auld;
My steps are frail, my een are bleared,
 My pow is unco bauld.
I've seen the snaws o' fourscore years
 O'er hill and meadow fa',
And, hinnie! were it no' for you,
 I'd gladly slip awa'

I feel I'm growing auld, gude-wife—
` I feel I'm growing auld;
Frae youth to age I've keepit warm
 The love that ne'er turned cauld.
I canna bear the dreary thocht
 That we maun sindered be;
There's naething binds my poor auld heart
 To earth, gude-wife, but thee.

I feel I'm growing auld, gude-wife—
 I feel I'm growing auld;

Life seems to me a wintry waste,
 The very sun feels cauld.
Of worldly friens ye've been to me,
 Amang them a' the best;
Now, I'll lay down my weary head,
 Gude-wife, and be at rest.

I CANNA LEAVE MY MINNIE.

BY JAMES LINEN.

Tak' back the ring, dear Jamie,
    The ring ye gae to me,
An' a' the vows ye made yestreen
    Beneath the birken tree.
But gie me back my heart again,
    It's a' I hae to gie;
Sin' ye'll no' wait a fittin' time,
    Ye canna marry me.

I promised to my daddie,
    Afore he slipp'd awa',
I ne'er wad leave my minnie,
    Whate'er sud her befa'.
I'll faithfu' keep my promise,
    For a' that ye can gie:
Sae, Jamie, gif ye winna wait,
    Ye ne'er can marry me.

I canna leave my minnie,
    She's been so kind to me
Sin' e'er I was a bairnie,
    A wee thing on her knee.
4*

Nae mair she'll caim my gowden hair,
    Nor busk me snod an' braw;
She's auld an' frail, her een are dim,
    An' sune will close on a'.

I maunna leave my minnie,
    Her journey is na long;
Her heid is bendin' to the mools
    Where it mun shortly gang.
Were I an heiress o' a crown,
    I'd a' its honors tine
To watch her steps in helpless age
    As she in youth watched mine.

THE WINTER SONG OF THE SHEP-HERD.

BY JAMES LINEN.

FAR out-ower the cauld muir, an' laigh in a
    howe,
  By a deep sleugh thro' whilk a burnie rins
    down,
Weel shielded frae storms by a heather-
    croun'd knowe,
  My sma' biggin stan's, wi' a fale-dyke
    aroun'.

What tho' down the lum-heid the flaucheatt
    fa' in,
  An' fizz for a jiffie where het the pessr
    lowe,
Snaw may drift, an' winds sough aroun' the
    bleak bin,
  The plooman o' care never furrows my
    brow.

The trees are a' leafless, the forests a' bare,
  The flowers are a' withered, an' Winter is
    here;

The bonnie wee robins my hamely meals
    share,
    That hap to my shielin an' think na o'
        fear.

I hae peats in the yard, an' hay in she mow,
    An' dizzens o' eggs that the chuckies hae
        laid;
A guid thumpin' kebbuck, a' soun' yet I
        trow,
    Save holes that some wee thievin' mousie
        has made.

The sheep in the fauld fin' eneuch for their
        mou',
    Ne'er toom is the draff-pock for Bessie
        the yad;
My ambry's weel stockit, my meal-buist is
        fu'—
    What mair needs a body to mak' the heart
        glad?

When at ora times thochtfu', I'm dowie an'
        wae
    Wi' thinkin' o' things that I canna weel
        name,

A wee drap o' barley-bree cheers me up sae,
  I feel like a laird in my strae-theekit hame.

There's Davoc the herd, the pluffy bit cal-
    lant,
  Wi' no a bane doxie about him ava,—
He'll blaw on the pipes, or croon an auld
    ballant,
  The lang nichts o' winter slip blithely
    awa'.

Fornent the peat-nuik, on a clean bed o'
    strae,
  The puir thing contented as onie lies
    doun;
He's up in the mornin' afore screich o' day,
  The image o' health—for his sleep has
    been soun'.

There's the collie foreby, my best frien' o'
    frien's,
  There's nae dog that wouffs half sae tentie
    as he;
Like mysel', for nae pampered bicker he
    griens,
  An' mornin' and nicht taks his crowdie
    wi' me.

When sheep loup the dikes, or rin aff frae
   the lave,
    Quick as stoure in a blast he's at their bit
      fuds;
When cauldly snaw-wreaths wad sune gie
   them a grave,
    To spare them out-owre the moss-muir-
      land he scuds.

The whaup braves the storm, the peesweip
   cries its name,
    An' aff to its covert the pairtraik may flee,
Sae, true to my nature, I naething mair
   claim
    Than providence kindly has ettled for me.

About braws an' siller I ne'er fash my thum,
    They breed yed an cares that I downa weel
      ken;
It's clear as the peat-reek that gaes up the
   lum,
    If thriftie, the maist o' folk aye mak a fen.

The spring time will come, and warm sunshine will bring,
    The ice-locket burnies flow gushin an'
      free;

The heather will bloom, an' the sweet linties
    sing,
  An' aff to the schaws a' the robins will
    flee.

Syne Simmer will come, clad in raiment o'
    green,
  The ewes an' their lammies will bleat on
    the lea,
The woods coral ring where no Winter is
    seen,
  An' gladness smile sweet on my wee hut
    an' me.

THE HILLS.

BY JOHN R. RIDGE.

I LOOK upon the purple hills,
　That rise in steps to yonder peaks,
And all my soul their silence thrills,
　And to my heart their beauty speaks.

What now to me the jars of life,
　Its petty cares, its harder throes?
The hills are free from toil and strife,
　And clasp me in their deep repose.

They soothe the pain within my breast,
　No power but their's could ever reach;
They emblem that eternal rest
　We cannot compass in our speech.

From far I feel their secret charm,
　From far they shed their healing balm,
And lost to sense of grief or harm,
　I plunge within their pulseless calm.

How full of peace and strength they stand,
　Self-poised and conscious of their weight!
We rise with them, that silent band,
　Above the wrecks of Time or Fate;

For, mounting from their depths serene,
　Their spirit pierces upward far,
A soaring pyramid serene,
　And lifts us where the angels are.

I would not lose this scene of rest,
　Nor shall its dreamy joy depart;
Upon my soul it is imprest,
　And pictured in my inmost heart.

THE HUMBOLDT DESERT.

BY JOHN R. RIDGE.

Who journeys o'er the desert now,
  Where sinks engulfed the Humboldt
      river,
Arrested in its sudden flow,
  But pouring in that depth forever.

As if the famished earth would drink
  Adry the tributes of the mountains,
Yet wither on the water's brink,
  And thirst for still unnumbered fountains.

Who journeys o'er that desert now
  Shall see strange sights, I ween, and
      ghastly;
For he shall trace, awearied, slow,
  Across this waste extended vastly,

The steps of pilgrims westward bound,
  Bound westward to the Land Pacific,
Where hoped-for rest and peace are found,
  And plenty waves her wand prolific.

Along this parched and dreary track,
　Nor leaf, nor blade, nor shrub appeareth;
The sky above doth moisture lack,
　And brazen glare the vision seareth;

Nor shadow, save the traveler's own,
　Doth bless with coolness seeming only,
And, save his muffled step alone
　Or desert-bird's wild shriek and lonely,

No sound is heard—a realm of blight,
　Of weird-like silence and a brightness
That maketh but a gloom of light,
　Where glimmer shapes of spectral white-
　　ness!

They are the bones that bleaching lie
　Where fell the wearied beast o'er-driven,
And upward cast his dying eye,
　As if in dumb appeal to heaven.

For lengthening miles on miles they lie,
　These sad memorials grim and hoary,
And every whitening heap we spy
　Doth tell some way-worn pilgrim's story.

Hard by each skeleton there stand
  The wheels it drew, or warped or shrunk-
    en,
And in the drifted, yielding sand
  The yoke or rusted chain lies sunken.

Nor marvel we, if yonder peers,
  From out some scooped-out grave and
    shallow,
A human head, which fleshless leers
  With look that doth the place unhallow.

Each annual pilgrimage hath strewn
  These monuments unnamed, undated,
Till now were bone but piled on bone,
  And heaped-up wrecks but congregated,

A pyramid would rise as vast
  As one of those old tombs Egyptian,
Which speak from distant ages past
  With time-worn, mystic, strange inscrip-
    tion.

But pass we these grim, mouldering things,
  Decay shall claim as Time may order,
For, offspring of the mountain springs,
  A river rims the desert border;

With margin green and beautiful,
   And sparkling waters silver-sounding,
And trees with zephyrs musical,
   And answering birds with songs abound-
      ing,

And velvet flowers of thousand scents,
   And clambering vines with blossoms
      crested;
Twas here the pilgrims pitched their tents,
   And from their toilsome travel rested.

Oh sweet such rest to him who faints
   Upon the journey long and weary!
And scenes like this the traveler paints,
   .While dying on the wayside weary.

Sad pilgrims o'er life's desert, *we,*
   Our tedious journey onward ever;
But rest for us there yet shall be,
   When camped upon the HEAVENLY
      RIVER.

MY LOST LOVE.

BY JOHN R. RIDGE.

I saw her when my heart was young,
  And she was beautiful and fair,
With silver music on her tongue,
  And golden glory in her hair,
And all love's glances round her flung,
  And Eve's first sweetness in her air.

I saw her 'mid the giddy throng,
  My bosom filled with wild romance;
'Twas she who sang the sweetest song,
  And she the stateliest in the dance.
Oh, could her heart to me belong,
  Her kisses warm my soul entrance!

I saw her by the wild-wood stream,
  Where swung the lilies tall and pale,
And roses kissed the sunny beam,
  And by their blushes told the tale—
And rose and lily (love the theme,)
  Upon her cheek did grow and fail.

"That rose's image in the wave,"
　　She said, "how sweet, reflected there!
Yet one rude gale it cannot brave,
　　But scattered all its beauties are."
"Its perfume still the flower shall save
　　Which lives on shore, and bless the air."

"It, too, shall pass," she sadly said,
　　I could not reason with her mood,
But felt the shadow of her dread
　　E'en in that summer solitude.
Oh heaven, shelter that dear head,
　　Tho' flowers may die in this lone wood.

I saw her when the dawning day
　　Was sculpturing from the silent night
Her white and stainless form; each ray
　　Revealed new raptures to my sight,
And, as the darkness fell away,
　　My arms enfolded all delight.

I saw her in another's arms!
　　Oh Death, within thy cold embrace—
The lily's blooms, the rose's charms
　　Affrighted from that fairest face.
Oh, cruel is the fate which harms
　　What God himself can ne'er replace.

I saw her next—alas, no more!
    How desolate a soul can be!
I wandered to the streamlet's shore,
    Nor rose, nor lily could I see;
Yet fell a voice: "To thee no more
    I come, but thou shalt come to me."

ARIADNE.

BY GEO. R. PARBURT.

DAUGHTER of Minos, king of ancient Crete,
  Whom Theseus did so lovingly adore;
It was most kind in thee, if not discreet,
  To teach him how to foil the Minotaur.

Love led thee to the labyrinth of death,
  Regardless of the mandates of thy sire,
To teach the young Athenian, with thy breath,
  Love's lessons—and escape the royal ire.

What if he were thy father's foe—and thine?
  Or justly doomed for crimes to make
    amends?
The love of maids is saint-like—so divine
  They love their enemies as well as friends.

Ah, Ariadne, those may blame who can;
  It was not for thy sex the Nazarene
Said, "Love your enemies," but for stern
    man,
  Who loves not even friends, when they're
    unseen.

5

Thou soughtest Theseus in the gloomy cave,
  And led him safely through its winding
      maze;
He bore thee off to Naxos—o'er the wave—
  All this was love—young love in virgin
      blaze.

Love taught him oft to vow he loved thee
      well!
  To weep and smile, when thou didst smile
      and weep,
To lead thee to a flowery, bridal dell,
  Then faithlessly desert thee—while asleep.

Wives oft sleep well, and find, when quite
      too late,
  Love both a labyrinth and minotaur;
For love, the wanton child of lust and fate,
  Can curse as wildly as it doth adore.

The stranger—Theseus—bound in chains, to
      thee
  An angel seemed—a maiden might set free;
The husband—Theseus—bounding o'er the
      sea,
  Was cursed full freely by his wife—by thee.

MY DIVINITY.

BY W. A. KENDALL.

Some Deity see in stars, some in the moon,
Some azure skies adore, or rising sun;
But I, more infidel than these—or wise—
   Worship alone thy orient eyes.

Naught see I more divine: to wood and
    stone,
And graven image I forego to kneel;
The redness of thy lips waylaying prayer,
    I can but falter, "Thou art fair!"

The silken tresses of thy hair enfold,
Like raven wings, the whiteness of thy breast;
Pearl tint and jet deliciously combine,
    To decorate my living shrine.

And when thy voice melodiously tunes
Itself to speech, and I the music hear,
My heart so thrills with rapture that I
    swoon,
    Losing the dulcet strain too soon.

Statues of marble, god and goddess wrought,
Half seen, half hid, through art's seductive
  - doors,
Invite approaches with immortal charms—
  I fly repellant to thy arms.

Diviner things may be, more high more
  pure—
The glory of their presence is not mine;
Thou art of Deity all that form can take,
  And I—am Pagan for thy sake.

Condemn me not for sacrilege, because
The fairest thing I see I deem divine;
Faith, like a rising feather backward blown,
  Is reconciled to the alone.

Richer, sweeter, nearer and dearer, are
Phrases I know not of, nor wish to learn;
Clasping thy alabaster waist, I swing
  The world round, daring everything!

Strewn upon western sunbeams' purple tints,
Bridals, and vows, and rings, like planet
  stars,
Sparkle along the night's dream-born abyss,
  As melts my orison into a kiss.

AM I WISE?

BY W. A. KENDALL.

While the sky is full of blue,
  And the flagon brims with red,
While the sun is full of brightness,
  And the stars beam overhead;
While the maids are fond and pretty,
  And the roses drip with dew,
I will pout my lips for kisses,
  Now be candid, would not you?

While the silk is soft and fine,
  And the sugar yields its sweet;
While the blooms come to the trees,
  And to ripeness swings the wheat;
While there's crimson in the sunset
  And freshness in the dawn;
I will give my heart to rapture
  In the face of dainty scorn!

While hope spans the radiant future,
  And whiteness clasps the truth;
While there's depth in every passion,
  And deliciousness in youth;

While the nights are dream-environed,
  And the days roll down in flame;
I will girdle them with transports,
  And will lift them up again!

While there's warmth in love's endear-
    ments
  And a tenderness in tears;
While there's symmetry in beauty,
  And in purple lapse the years;
While new pleasures bud before me,
  Though the old ones fade and fall;
I will still persist in wooing,
  Till I'm wedded to them all!

Till hearts cease to throb together,
  And white arms refuse to twine;
Till full lips refuse to answer,
  And the grapes deny me wine;
Till all colors run to blackness,
  And all bubbles cease to rise,
I will not cast down joy's chalice;
  Is that otherwise than wise?

This I deem is primal wisdom:
  Plant to-day and pluck the fruit;

All the morrows are full-handed,
  All the yesterdays are mute;
Every day some blessings ripen,
  Every day some blessings rot;
Shake them down as you pass under
  And you'll find no barren spot!

Does the sun restrain his glory,
  Fearing future time will lack?
Do the clouds retain their moisture,
  Lest the earth should give none back?
No! they lend with loyal largeness
  To the present moment's need;
Trusting that the growing harvest
  Will requite them with its seed.

Put your sickle in, O, reaper!
  There are other fields beyond;
Use the good the chances offer,
  Thriftless thrift that does despond;
Bend and glean amid the plenty,
  Get and give with equal hand;
Growth is constant, and enjoyment
  Fills the measure of demand.

A MID-SUMMER AFTERNOON.

BY W. A. KENDALL.

Beneath the vine-clad porch I sit entranced,
  The while the westering noon-tide ebbs
    away;
Immobile hills recline haze-wrapped against
  The sultry limits of the yellow day.

I know the star-cowled night, with dusky
    feet,
  Is on the trail of glory—yet I dream;
Imperial asters doze adown the walk,
  And fragrant pinks, lethargic, nod astream.

And this is passion-time's serene content—
  Here in the Summer's ample lap I lie,
Bathed with the warmth of her exotic breath,
  Lulled by the passive music of her sigh.

And she is grand, in this, her tropic mood;
  Grand as the Queen of a voluptuous isle,
Where forms are round and tempting, and
    where mouths
  Are luscious centres of perpetual smile.

And thus the wanton Summer loiters by,
  While in exquisite drunk'ness I recline,
Quaffing her essences at every sense,
  Clasping her round with ravishments di-
    vine.

The fountains plash, the coy winds fan the
    leaves;
  A misty languor of expectant bliss
Pervades the earth, the air, the sea, the
    sky—
  I think of ripe lips thirsting for a kiss.

Oh, balmy draught, poured from a thousand
    founts
  Of rare enjoyment!—whence this taste of
    rue?
I see, and seeing, sigh—the day is dead!
  And all the world is bathed in tears of dew.

The vesper-shadows from the swarthy east,
  In sables tipped with ermine lustres rise;
And, as they troop, lo!—like a signal torch
  The Evening Star gleams in the western
    skies.

5*

Unnumbered silver lamps through space are
    hung,
  Lit at the altar of some brighter sphere;
And as the dim Earth, conscious, darkles on,
  A tranquil ray finds on my cheek a tear.

Wrap me in blossom-scents serene and cool,
  Lay me to dream with aromatic Night;
And if it be of love, or be of scorn,
  Oh, wake me not till flames the Solar
    Light.

TOGETHER.

BY J. F. BOWMAN.

I cannot save thee,—we must die,—but when
  The stifling waves shall coldly close above
Our sinking forms, my steadfast eyes even
      then,
  Shall turn to thine with love.

Thus,—folded in the last,—*the last* embrace,
  The cruel flood shall drink our failing
      breath,
Thus,—gazing fondly in the well-loved face,
  We shall be one in death.

'Twill soon be over, sweet! 'Tis not so hard
  As our fears paint it. Gladly would I
      bear
All thou wilt suffer in that final pang
  We must together share.

See these distracted ones, who weep and rave,
  In ghastly terror, whose despairing cries,
Out-shriek the storm, and wildly against Fate,
  In frantic protest rise.

They trebly die; theirs is an agony
   That souls upborne by love can never
      share,
No such ignoble pangs for thee and me! .
   Calm, even in despair.

And while the giant demon, pallid Fear,
   With icy spell each palsied heart con-
      trols,
Lo! we can smile in the fixed face of Death—
   The tyrant of weak souls.

Though the lip quivers and the cheek grows
      pale,
   Still in thy steadfast and confiding eye,
Is promise of a heart that will not fail,
   Till breathes the latest sigh.

For we can look beyond this hour of dread,
   With a faith born of love that cannot
      die,
And feel in our own hearts, the perfect
      pledge
   Of Immortality.

See,   the   bow   settles   for   the   downward
    plunge,
  Close,   closer   to   my   heart!—that   fearful
    cry!
"We   sink,   we   sink!"   One   kiss,   on   earth
    the   last!
  Now   farewell,   earth   and   sky.

HOMESICK.

BY J. F. BOWMAN.

They may talk of the cloudless heaven,
    Of "this land of the flag and the vine;"
Of her valleys and crested mountains,
    And her climate almost divine.
They may talk of the mines and vineyards
    Of "our glorious land of gold."
Of oil-wells, and feet, and quartz claims,
    Which are bought by fools who are sold.

But give me the land of my boyhood,
    Where the seasons come and go;
Where the Spring brings the rains of April,
    And the Winter brings ice and snow;
Where Summer comes panting and breath-
        less,
    Where the robin and bob-o-link sing;
And the woods are appareled in Autumn,
    More gorgeously than a king.

Where friends are still gentle and loyal,
    And lovers are tender and true;

Where old ties are piously cherished,
  Not carelessly sundered for new;
Where youth is retiring and modest,
  And age is respected and wise;
And the hearts of the home-nurtured mai-
    dens
  Are as pure as the blue of their eyes.

Where still like a smooth-flowing river,
  Glides the peaceful current of life—
Not with the wild rush of a torrent,
  In turmoil, and tumult and strife;
Where the mind and the heart have treas-
    ures,
  That cannot be bought or sold,
Yet are held with a wealth more precious,
  Than the usurer's hoarded gold.

Once more I see the old homestead,
  That stands at the end of the lane,
And the feelings of childhood all freshly
  Come back with that vision again.
And I yearn for the land where each season
  In its turn appeareth the best,
And where life in its striving and turmoil,
  Has a flavor of sweetness and rest.

AT THE BALL.

BY J. F. BOWMAN.

The music swells, the dancers move,
  The laugh and jest go gaily round,
But ah! my truant fancies rove
  And scarce I hear the festive sound.
I think of one who far away,
  Is numbered with the patriot band,
Whose hearts perchance have bled to-day,
  For Freedom and their Native Land.

The music throbs with pulse more strong—
  Once *he* was foremost in the dance,
And none could boast in pleasure's throng
  A lighter foot, a blither glance.
But when the storm of battle burst,
  And treason bared the ready brand,
His sword leaped forth among the first
  For Freedom and his Native Land.

And still as on my absent ear
  The music falls with louder swell,
I seem the cannon's boom to hear—
  The hissing shot, the shrieking shell!

Even while the giddy waltz reels by,
　In battle's front I see him stand;
Heaven guard my hero while he strikes,
　For Freedom and his Native Land!

MADRIGAL.

BY CHARLES WARREN STODDARD.

A MAID is seated by a brook,
　The sweetest of sweet creatures;
I pass that way with my good book,
But cannot read, nor cease to look
　Upon her winsome features.

Amongst the blushes on her cheek
　Her small white hand reposes,
I am a shepherd, for I seek
That willful lamb, with fleece so sleek,
　Feeding among the roses.

A RHYME OF LIFE.

BY CHARLES WARREN STODDARD.

IF life is as a flame that death doth kill,
   Burn little candle lit for me,
With a pure spark, that I may rightly see
   To word my song, and utterly
      God's plan fulfill.

If life is as a flower that blooms and dies,
   Forbid the cunning frost that slays
With Judas kiss, and trusting life betrays;
   Forever may my voice of praise
      Untainted rise!

If life is as a voyage, or foul, or fair,
   Oh! bid me not my banners furl
For adverse gale, or wave in angry whirl,
   Till I have found the gates of pearl,
      And anchored there.

THE WOODPECKER.

BY CHARLES WARREN STODDARD.

A busy woodpecker! what would you call
  This monk of a fellow, tapping a tree,
With little cells like a catacomb-hall,
To bury his acorns in; what would you call
  Such a curious monk as he?

Tucking his acorns away in their tomb,
  To feed upon by-and-by at his will—
Does he ever think of the hidden bloom
In the acorn's heart? though shut in a tomb
  There's a germ of life nursed there still!

Time is a woodpecker, crowding the cells
  Of the catacomb earth with holy dead;
But there is a bud of life that swells
In the oak-tree's might, and it shatters the
      cells
  As the soul when the life has fled.

THE WILL OF GOD IS ACCOM-
PLISHED: AMEN.

BY CHARLES WARREN STODDARD.

"THERE is a city beyond the sea,
With the gates of pearl and the pave of gold;
Out of the night of gloom are we,
Out of the mist of tears:
Captain, I leave the ship with thee,
For the holy breath of God will fold
The ripples before thee. Seek the gate
That is formed of a single pearl, and wait
The angel that beareth the golden key;
Not an evil thing shall pass with thee,
Never a thought of fears.

You cannot miss the haven of hope,
With God at the helm, and angel's wings
Puffing the sail with their flutterings,
And a loyal soul at every rope."

"God be with you, captain and crew!"
Said the pilot kindly. Every one
Cried "Amen, pilot! God bless you!"
"A prosperous voyage has just begun;

I have another work to do;
 God be with you!"   Then, like a light,
 The pilot's soul went out with the night.
We were alone, but our chart was true,
 On we sped with the rising sun.
Why did the pilot's guiding cease?
He had found *Heaven:* we had found *peace.*

QUITS.

BY C. H. WEBB.

SHE is dead! and they say for her fame
    It was barely in time that she died;
Better thus—she could never brook shame—
    For oh! she had terrible pride.

Sure the path to the grave was soon trod—
    She is resting, and so let it be;
But why do the gossips all nod,
    And point with their fingers at me?

That a sin is not buried, they tell,
    Though the sexton dig deep as he can;
Perhaps it was murder: ah! well,
    Let God be my judge—not man.

For she mocked me at first, when I came
    To fling a young heart at her feet,
And she spurned me, because of a shame
    That was done ere my pulses had beat.

Her birth, so she said, had no stain—
　　She was one of a noble old line,
And the blood that flowed red in her veins
　　Could not mingle with current like mine.

On the world's brow I wrote me a name,
　　Fair cheeks flashed with pride at my tread;
Then I wooed her with gold and with fame—
　　I wooed, but I wooed not to wed.

I remember her speech—it was fine,
　　That the house of her sire had no stain;
By my faith, of that same noble line
　　That boast will be made not again!

It was murder?   Well, well, let it rest;
　　I will answer myself for the deed;
All tears are weak brine at the best,
　　And prayer serves all knaves in their need

Vex me not, shaven priest, stand apart!
　　Dole thy tedious texts out to fools;
For I swear there is that in my heart
　　Just now that would puzzle the schools.

Of your future I reck not a toss—
    Earth has torments that hell cannot give!
There's a grave where the four roads cross—
    She is dead, and I—I ?—I live !

6

"I ALWAYS COVERED MOTHER."

THE DAUGHTER AT THE GRAVE.

BY C. H. WEBB.

I HAVE always covered mother,
  Since the pain came to her brow,
And she said I did it gently—
  None else shall do it now.

I have always smoothed her pillow,
  And drawn the curtain-fold;
And I'll not forget thee now, mother,
  When thy limbs are all so cold.

'Neath the willows, deep and narrow,
  They have made thy bed, I know,
Yet they shall not soil thy robes, mother,
  With the damp earth-mould below.

See, I've plucked some wild flowers,
      mother,
  And I'll strew them on thy breast,
And the buds shall fall so gently
  That they may not break thy rest.

I'd bring thee brighter flowers, mother,
    But the roses fled with June,
And the daisies and anemones
    Went with the sweet May moon.

But the buds fell from the stem, mother,
    To be caught by hands on high—
Now they blossom in God's garden
    Pale lilies of the sky.

And 'tis thus with souls like thine, mother,
    For they pass from life to love;
And they leave this dark earth-garden
    For the golden walks above.

Oh, the sweet star-lilies blossom
    Where no hand may pluck them down,
Or I'd weave, to grace thy brow, mother,
    A purer, fairer crown.

But the angels' wings are free, mother,
    And you can wander there,
Where the flowers are blooming ever,
    With a fragrance like to prayer.

Now the counterpane is spread, mother,
    You'll wake to morning light—
God's hand has drawn the curtain,
    So, mother, sweet, good-night!

SONNET. .

BY C. H. WEBB.

LAST night, in blue my little love was drest;
  And as she walked the room in maiden
     grace,
I looked into her fair and smiling face,
  And said that blue became my darling best.
But when, next morn, a snowy virgin vest
  And robe of white did the blue one dis-
     place,
She seemed a pearl-tinged cloud—and I was
     space;
  She filled my soul as cloud-forms fill the
     west.
And so it is, that changing day by day—
  Changing her robe, but not her loveliness,
Whether the gown be blue or white or gray,
  I deem that one the most becoming dress;
The truth is this: in any robe or way,
  I love her just the same, and cannot love
     her less.

LOVE ME, DARLING!

BY A. M'KAW BURR.

Love me, darling of my soul,
Ceaseless as the billows roll!
  As response to my devotion,
  Grant me dear, love's deep emotion!
Love me, Queen of purity,
As my soul now yearns for thee,
  For I languish mournful-hearted,
  Each sad moment from thee parted ;
    Love me, darling, love me long,
    Is the burden of my song!
      Love me not platonic, merely,
      Love me warmly, love me dearly!
    With emotion don't be chary,
    Love me, darling, love me, Mary.

Love me, darling, may our bond
Be the soul's emotions fond!
  Faint with hope my heart is aching,
  For thy fervent love 'tis breaking!
Love me when the glowing sun
Starts his daily course to run!

Love me at the hour of even,
Changing gloomy earth to heaven!
   Love me, darling, love me long,
   Is the burden of my song
      Love me not platonic, merely,
      Love me warmly, love me dearly!
   With emotion don't be chary!
   Love me, darling, love me, Mary!

Love me, darling, jewel rare,
None with lovely form so fair!
   All aglow my heart is burning,
   For thy fondest love 'tis yearning!
Love me, Queen of all that's true,
Purest of the angel few—
   Cheering on the sad and lonely,
   Love me, darling, love me, only!
      Love me, darling, love me long,
      Is the burden of my song!
         Love me not platonic, merely,
         Love me warmly, love me dearly!
      With emotion don't be chary,
      Love me, darling, love me Mary!

THREE YEARS.

APRIL, 1864.

BY JOSEPH T. GOODMAN.

How move the tides of great events,
    Which thro' the nation ebb and flow,
Since from Fort Sumter's battlements
    The Banner fell, three years ago?
I hear the battle-surges beat,
    I mark the clash of sword and lance,
I watch the onset and retreat;
And still through triumph and defeat,
    I see the glorious flag advance!

As beautiful and bright as first,
    That starry Banner still appears,
Unscathed by treason's angry burst,
    And battle-tempests of three years!
And never waved it prouder, grander,
    Than in the dreadful trial hour,
Disdaining ever to surrender
One gleam of its old heavenly splenaor,
    One right of its old earthly power!

Ah, never banner yet unfurled
   In cause so holy and sublime!
We fight the Battle of the World,
   We make the Conquest of all Time—
The battle of the deathless Free,
   The conquest of eternal Right:
A million bayonets we see,
But unseen million blades there be
   Of God's own angels in the fight.

Think not the world moves laggardly,
   Or that events are marching slow;
'Twere well to let an age roll by,
   If one great blessing marked its flow.
Seven years our fathers toiled in pain,
    Till Freedom's birth-hour came at
      length ;
If need, what faint-heart shall complain
That seven long years we fight again
    To guard that Freedom's life and
      strength !

The grand events of time alway
    Have been brought forth in travail
      long ;
'Tis not the labor of a day
    To do away a century wrong ;

6*

When centuries of idle tears
    Have mourned a wrong of toil and
        pains,
'Tis work enough for three short years,
For e'en a million volunteers
    To cut apart four million chains.

Bear on the Banner, with its folds
    By fiery tempests scorched and torn!
Through every rent mine eye beholds,
    In brighter glory, battle-born,
A land whose boast of liberty
    Is not the scorn of million slaves—
A nation that is truly free,
And swears that it will ever be
    By all its heroes' sacred graves!

AT THE GATE.

BY JOSEPH T. GOODMAN.

In dreamy languor, through the tasseled
    pines,
The crescent moon lay in the hazy west;
Above the gateway clung the trellised vines;
    My arms twined gently round her neck
    and breast.

The vine-leaves tittered at the tender wooing
    Of love-lorn breezes from the balmy south;
Soft floods of tresses o'er my cheek fell flow-
    ing,
    A breath ambrosial sweetly bathed my
    mouth.

A tremulous ray shone deep down in her eyes,
    The star-light wanders in a vague eclipse;
Then leaves and breezes sobbed out envious
    sighs,
    As slowly parted our reluctant lips.

POEM.

BY JOSEPH T. GOODMAN.

A NATION lay at rest. The mighty storm
That threatened their good ship with direful
    harm
. Had spent its fury; and the tired and worn
Sank in sweet slumber as the spring-time
    morn
Dawned with a promise that the strife should
    cease,
And War's grim face smiled in a dream of
    peace.

O, doubly sweet the sleep when tranquil light
Breaks on the dangers of the fearful night,
And full of trust, we seek the dreamy realm,
Conscious a faithful pilot holds the helm,
Whose steady purpose and untiring hand,
With God's good grace, will bring us safe to
    land.

And so the nation rested, worn and weak
From long exertion—
                    God! what a shriek
Was that which pierced to farthest earth and
    sky,
As though all Nature uttered a death-cry!
Awake! arouse! ye sleeping wardens, ho!
Be sure this augurs some colossal woe;
Some dire calamity has passed o'erhead—
A world is shattered, or a god is dead!

What! the globe unchanged?   The sky still
    specked
With stars?   Time is?   The universe not
    wrecked?
Then look ye to the pillars of the State!
How fares it with the nation's good and
    great?
Since that wild shriek told no unnatural birth,
Some mighty soul has shaken hands with
    earth.

Lo! murder has been done!   Its purpose
    foul
Hath stained the marble of the capitol!
Where sat one yesterday without a peer,
Still rests he peerless—but upon his bier!

Ah, faithful heart, so silent now—alack!
And did the nation fondly call thee back,
And hail thee truest, greatest of the land,
To bare thy breast to the assassin's hand?
And yet we know if that extinguished voice
Could be rekindled, and pronounce its choice
Between this awful fate of thine, and one
Retreat from what thou didst or would have
          done
In thine own sense of duty, it would choose
This doom—the least a noble soul could lose!

There is a time when the assassin's knife
Kills not, but stabs into eternal life:
And this was such a one.   Thy homely name
Was wed to that of Freedom, and thy fame
Hung rich and clustering in its lusty prime;
The God of heroes saw the harvest-time,
And smote the noble structure at the root,
That it might bear no less immortal fruit!

Sleep! honored by the nation and mankind!
Thy name in history's proudest page is
          shrined,
Adorned by virtues only, and shall exist
Bright and adored on Freedom's martyr list.

The time shall come when on the Alps will
    dwell
No memory of their own immortal Tell;
Rome shall forget her Cæsars, and decay
Waste the Eternal City's self away;
And in the lapse of countless ages, Fame
Shall one by one forget each cherished name;
But thine shall live through time, until there
    be
No soul on earth that glories to be free!

TOM DARLING.

●

BY L. F. WELLS.

TOM DARLING was a darling Tom,
   (Excuse all vulgar puns;)
A type of California's bright
   Rising and setting suns.

His father was an austere man—
   An oyster man was he,
Who opened life by opening
   The shell-fish of the sea;

But hearing of a richer clime,
   He took his only son,
And came where golden minds are lost,
   While golden mines are won.

They hoped to fill their pockets from
   Rich pockets in the ground;
And 'midst the boulders of the hills,
   None bolder could be found.

For though a mining minor, Tom
   Was never known to shirk;

And while with zeal he worked his claim,
  His father claimed his work.

Time's record on his brow now showed
  A fair and spotless page;
And, as his age became him well,
  He soon became of age.

Thinking that he was up to all
  The California tricks,
He now resolved to pick his way
  Without the aid of picks. .

In less than eighteen circling moons
  Two fortunes he had made;
One by good luck at trade in stock,
  And one by stock in trade.

With health and wealth he now could live
  Upon the easy plan;
While every body said of course,
  He was a fine young man.

But Thomas fell, and sadly too,
  Who of his friends would 'thought it?
He ran for office, and alas!
  For him and his—he caught it.

Mixing no more with sober men,
  He found his morals fleeing;
And being of a jovial turn,
  He turned a jovial being.

With governor and constable
  His cash he freely spends;
From constable to governor,
  . He had a host of friends.

But soon he found he could not take,
  As his old father would,
A little spirits, just enough .
  To do his spirits good.

In councils with the patriots
  Upon affairs of State,
Setting no bars to drinking, he
  Soon lost his upright gait.

His brandy straightway made him walk
  In very crooked ways;
While lager beer brought to his view
  A bier and span of grays.

·The nips kept nipping at his purse—
  (Two bits for every dram,)

While clear champagne produced in him
    A pain that was no sham.

His cups of wine were followed by
    The doctor's painful cup;
Each morning found him getting low
    As he was getting up.

Thus uselessly, and feebly did
    His short existence flit,
Till in a drunken fight he fell
    Into a drunken fit.

The doctors came, but here their skill
    They found of no avail;
They all agreed, what ailed poor Tom
    Was politics and ale.

MARY BROWN.

BY L. F. WELLS.

SHE dwelt where the long wintry showers
   Hold undisputed sway,
Where frowning April drives the flowers
   Far down the lane of May—
A simple, rustic child of song,
   Reared in a chilling zone,
The idol of a household throng—
   The cherished one of home.
None sang her praise, or heard her fame
   Beyond her native town;
She bore no fancy-woven name,
   'Twas simply Mary Brown.

Her eyes were not a shining black,
   Nor yet a heavenly blue,
They might be hazel, or, alack—
   Some less poetic hue;
Indeed I mind me, long ago,
   One pleasant summer day,
A passing stranger caught their glow,
   I think he called them gray,

Yet when with earnestness they burned,
　Till other eyes grew dim,
Their outward tint was ne'er discerned—
　The spell was from within.

A novelist with fancy's pen,
　Would scarcely strive to trace
From her a fairy heroine
　Of matchless mien and grace;
A model for the painter's skill,
　Or for the sculptor's art,
Her form might not be called, yet still
　It bore a gentle heart.
The while it fondly treasured long
　Love's lightest whispered tone,
In other hearts she sought·no wrong,
　She knew none in her own.

Though never skilled in fashion's school,
　To sweep the trembling keys,
Or strike the harp by studied rule,
　A listening throng to please ;
Yet still, when anguish rent the soul,
　And fever reached the brain,
Her fingers knew the skillful touch
　Which soothed the brow of pain,

And widow's thanks, and orphan tears
    Had owned her tender care,
While little children gathered near,
    Her earnest love to share.

I might forget the queenly dame
    Of high and courtly birth,
Descending from an ancient name
    Among the sons of earth;
I scarce recall the dazzling eyes
    Of her, the village belle,
Who caused so many rural sighs
    From rustic hearts to swell;
Yet never can I cease to own
    While future years shall roll
Thy passing beauty, Mary Brown,
    The beauty of thy soul.

"TRULY YOURS,
EVER THE SAME."

BY HUGH HUMPHREY.

"Ever the same," so the letter said.
  I thought of the writer and blessed her
    dear name,
As over and over the missive I read,
  Till I came to the close, which was, "Ever
    the same."

"Ever the same." That sad April eve
  Comes to me often, when clasped to my
    heart
I kissed her, my darling I soon was to leave,
  While she mournfully murmured, "O,
    why must we part?"

Ever the same? The death angel waved
  Over her pathway his mantle of fate.
O, the deep sorrow of worshiping friends,
  Watching her course to the shadowy gate!

Who is it kneeling the death-bed beside?
  Hark! she is whispering, calling his name.
"Henry, I hoped to have been thy own
    bride,
  But up there in heaven I'll love thee the
    same."

Ah! was she false? A question I ask
  Always and ever; though never.I'll know
Whether or not she was wearing a mask.
  Ah! the Hereafter, what secrets will show.

Here goes for a fire! I think a light
  Will tend to lesson somewhat this gloom,
By chasing away the ghosts of night,
  The flitting shadows that haunt the room.

Gone, all gone! and with it, I trust,
  Every thought of the frail and the fair.
And she too is gone; may her judgment be
    just:
  And the letter is gone, but the ashes are
    there.

A CURIOUS LEGEND.

BY HUGH HUMPHREY.

"Tell me a story," sweet Carrie said,
As she laid her little hand in mine;
Tell me a story—some thrilling tale
Of a lovely lady, tall and pale,
And a valiant knight in burnished mail
With a hated rival to assail—
  Tell me a story, cousin, mine.

The sunlight through the open blinds
  Fell on her wavy, golden hair;
And I thought never a Norman dame
Or Saxon maid could ever claim
Such beauty as did my heart inflame.
  And I answered, "Listen, cousin fair."

In an ancient, yellow book, I read
Of those who for ages have long been dead;

Of pages and knights and earls,
Of Norman lords and Saxon churls;

Of a murdered monk, and a sheeted ghost—
But this was the legend that pleased me most.

7

Young Eginardus, I think, was the name
Of a handsome page of goodly frame,
In the court of some ancient, feudal king,
Who had a daughter—a common thing
In those early days.   And this young girl,
As lovely a lady as ever a curl
Of rippling gold did ever grace,
Had fallen in love with the pretty face
Of Eginardus; and he, no doubt,
Was not very long in finding it out.
       Of course, you know
       It wasn't the thing
       For the child of a king, .
Her love to bestow on a hireling.

•But Eginardus was rash and bold—
Young fellows in love often are, I am told.
And so by stealth they met at night
In the princess' chamber:—It wasn't right;
And, like the crimes of a prowling thief,
Was pretty sure to bring them to grief.
"The best-laid plans will sometimes fail,"
As the burglar said when returned to jail.
One night through the chill and frosty air,
Across the courtyard and up the stair

With noiseless step Eginardus crept
To the room where his loving princess slept.
      An hour was spent
      In the arms of bliss,
      With many a kiss;—
Ah! little he thought there was aught amiss.

As the golden moments onward flew,
The courtyard was changing its sombre hue,
Softly and silently below
Was spread a carpet of pure snow,
And when had ended their interview,
How to get back he hardly knew!
Some awkward places I've seen in my day,
But nothing like that, I can safely say.
O, Eginardus! thou'dst better kept
Away from the room where the princess
    slept!
Though every door be unlocked and un-
    barred,
How can you cross the snow in the yard?
      I say it with shame,
      Alas! alack!
      To cover his track,
The princess carried him on her back.

Little they thought, how with fearful frown,
The king, from his chamber looking down,
Beheld it all.   A tyrant's head
Uneasily rests on his couch, 'tis said—
And that was the reason at that late hour
The king looked forth from his guarded
    tower.
How the monarch stamped on the oaken
    floor,
How he ground his teeth, how he cursed
    and swore,
How he vengeance vowed, and a great deal
    more,
I've not time to tell; yet I have no doubt
His talk was by no means very devout.
        The very next day
        The herald's call
        Summoned them all
To meet in the royal council hall.

Knights and squires and ladies fair,
The page and the princess, all were there.
The king rehearsed the wondrous tale—
The page and the princess both grew pale.
"The doom of him," the old king cried,
"Who thus degraded a royal bride?"

Death! was the cry, that rose above
The princess' pleading of truest love.
And the legend here goes on to show,
After days of grief and nights of woe,
How the king forgave them both, and the
     page
Became a lord in that feudal age.
        The book don't say,
        Yet 'tis very plain
        That the happy twain
As lord and lady in love did reign.
Of curious tales there were quite a host,
But this was the legend that pleased me
    most.

THE MERCHANT'S SOLILOQUY.

BY HUGH HUMPHREY.

I searched for a missing deed last night
    And the deed I could not find;
But a yellow letter came to light,
    Which brought old scenes to mind
            Again,
    Which brought old scenes to mind.

It was long ago when you wrote that page
    A long, long time ago;
I was young myself; and you?—your age
    Was just sixteen you know
            Rowene,
    Was just sixteen you know.

Ah, yes! those were pleasant times, I'll own,
    When the world seemed free from guile.
I am wiser now, for I long have known
    The worth of a woman's smile,
            Rowene,
    The worth of a woman's smile.

Do you ever think of the misty past,
   Of our walks to the "Old Sunset?"
Of your smiles and tears as my hand you
      clasped
   The tricks of an arch-coquette,
            Rowene,
   The tricks of an arch-coquette.

It is over now; but this yellow page
   Brought back the buried past.
We were both to young, I can see it now,
   For our love to ever last,
            Rowene,
   For our love to ever last.

THE VILLAGE BELL.

BY RALPH KEELER.

PEALED the ancient village bell
Over distant mead and dell,
From the church upon the hill,
On the Sunday morning still,
Calling to the pews of oak
All the honest village folk.

And among the simple throng
Little Mary walked along,
With her tiny dimpled hand
In her mother's, hard and tanned,
Prattling crystal, childish words,
How she wondered that the birds,
Little truants of the bowers,
Dared to sing in Sabbath hours.

Happy in her mother's love,
Rich in wealth she knew not of;
Rubies shutting over curls
Were her lips and teeth ; her curls
Waving richly fold on fold,
Filagree of purest gold,

Pealed again the village bell
Over distant mead and dell,
From the church upon the hill,
On a summer morning still,
Calling to the pews of oak
. Merry trains of village folk.

And among the bridal throng,
Mary, blushing, walked along,
Clasping tightly to a hand—
Not her mother's—hard and tanned,
Lisping coyish, maiden words;
While again the little birds,
Merry minstrels of the bowers,
Poured their melodies in showers.

Pealed again the village bell,
Over hamlet, mead and dell,
And among the funeral throng,
Mary, pale, was borne along.
Cold upon her quiet breast,
Folded were her hands in rest.

And the birds, still tiring never,
Sing their minstrel songs forever.
Peals again the village bell,
Mary used to love so well,

Pounding at the gates of night,
Tolling darkness into light.

Preaching with its mellow tongue,
Homilies to old and young;
Telling tales of joy or woe,
To the dead who rest below;
Giving back the love she gave—
Does she hear it in the grave?

AT THE PLAY.

BY RALPH KEELER.

I saw her at the play last night; she sat
By one I knew she did not love, and I
By one who was, she knew, as naught to me.
Our glances met midway, and struggling fell,
All shattered by the bastioned wall that pride
Had reared against the years when we were all
To one another. 'Twas a simple play—
A story of a long, long constancy;
Of truth that was too tender to be told;
Hope that clung, crumbling with the years
    deferred,
The ivy to the ruin of itself;
And a long life that had gone out in sighing.

And when the hero in the scene had said
"And we have known each other all our lives,
And I have loved you better than you knew,"
Our glances met again. My heart thrilled
    with
A pain that was akin to gladness—
A bitter-sweet of memory and of hope.

Her eye was wet, and we both knew it was
No mimic scene to us. .

The play was over.   We went each our way
Back to the coldness we had known so long.
Our hearts, like friends who have spent years
       .in search,
Had met and passed each other in the crowd.
Alas! the power of pride.   Oh, it hath made
More exiles than the laws; for it alone
Can make a weary exile of the heart.

MADGE.

BY RALPH KEELER.

My Madge was twelve, and I fourteen,
  We loved like angels in Tom Moore;
We vowed such vows as ne'er had been,
  In rhymes or moon-light made before.

A lustrum passed, and she was small;
  And I, a stripling, still was smaller;
And Madge, forgetting vows and all,
  Went off and married Joseph Lawler.

She spoke about "the boy," and grieved
  That one so clever wasn't taller;
While she, the merest tendril cleaved
  About the oak of Joseph Lawler.

And thus it was my griefs began,
  And I have borne them like a Roman;
How long it takes to be a man,
  How very short to be a woman!

A SONG FOR US ALL.

BY R. F. GREELEY.

Sing us a carol, Amy, *ma belle*,
Sing me the song that we loved so well,
When our group was full and our hearts
    were light,
And visions of transport crowned the night.

I will sing you a song, young brother mine,
But not the carol of "auld lang syne,"
For our hearts are tombs that dear forms
    inclose,
And sad were the breaking of their repose.

I will sing you rather of what shall be
When our flag is dreaded on every sea,
And the wine-press running with vintage o'er,
Shall emblem the plenty that lies before.

I hear the tramp of unnumbered feet,
I see the bonfires in every street,
I hear the din of that myriad shout
That shall thrill the world when our quarrel's
    out.

Gleaming on many a hill-side green,
Where the tall wheat waves in its golden
    sheen,
Many 's the white-walled cot I see
Made gay by the pranks of infancy.

Yon dell where no spade disturbed the soil,
Shall ring the song of the sons of toil,
And the cannon covered with rust shall stand
By the roadside to guide the emigrant band,
Tramping along to the silver land.

Under the vine, under the vine,
Yet we shall gather, fair brother mine,
And such notes of war as may roll from far
Will be lost in the tread-loom's ceaseless jar.

Ply the shuttle, and speed the plough,
Merrily scale the mountain's brow,
Gather the treasures of furrow and field—
For treason's doom is fairly sealed.

My carol is sung, fair brother mine,
Is it not better than "auld lang syne?"
For it tells not of carnage and battle glee,
But a better time that is yet to be.

NIGHT AMONG THE MOUNTAINS.

BY R. F. GREELEY.

TWILIGHT lingers o'er the landscape,
  And the life-bestowing sun,
Putting on his crimson mantle,
  Tells the world that day is done.

Purple mists enshroud the valley,
  Though a single ray doth lie
On those bare and rock-bound summits,
  Boldly marked against the sky

'Gainst whose glittering escutcheon,
  Since the natal day of Time,
Rocks that dared the storm for ages,
  Stand in solitude sublime.

High and hoar above the landscape
  Slowly fading from the sight,
Looking down on hill and hamlet,
  They await the coming night.

Deeper fall the evening shadows,
  Till at length the heavenly maze
Seems a half-transparent curtain,
  Pierced by countless golden rays.

From the world of gloom that lingers
  In the narrow pass below,
Comes the sound of rushing waters
  In their wild and headlong flow,

And the light of Indian fires,
  In the distance dimly seen,
Casts a glow upon the bosom
  Of the tide that rolls between.

Rugged pines that rise majestic
  From the ravines dim and dark,
Shroud the scene in gloom unfathomed ;
  Now the wolf doth howl,—and hark !

Through the canon comes a cadence,
  Rising, falling evermore,—
'Tis the breeze that blends its voices
  With the torrent's muffled roar,

Leaping down through cleft and chasm
  With a motion wild and free,
Till it mingles with the waters
  Rolling onward to the sea.

Look! where in the farther distance,
  Glittering on the brow of night
Like some rare, resplendent jewel,
  The Sierra looms to sight—

Monarch of the western border,
  Crowned with eternal snow!
Him the sun first greets at morning,
  Last on him the moon doth glow;

And beneath us in the valley,
  Flickering lights peep dimly out
From the low and leafy covert,
  Where the miner holds his rout;

Merry notes of flute and fiddle,
  Echo to the mountain air,
Stamping feet and laughing voices
  Making mockery of care.

Yes—in many a boarded cabin,
　Rude and cheerless to the sight,
Peace and measureless contentment
　Visit many a breast to-night.

Where beside the crackling fagot,
　With the best of mountain cheer,
Rests the miner from his labor—
　And life's troubles disappear.

CHRISTMAS.

BY J. WINANS.

CHRISTMAS is coming! there's life in the
    sound
Of Time's fleeting coursers, that o'er the
    crisp ground,
Are dashing and clattering—reckless of rest—
To bring to our borders the right welcome
    guest.
For Christmas, glad Christmas, warm greet-
   .ings be given,
The time-honored stranger, bluff, hearty and
    strong;
Dull care for a while from each bosom be
    driven,
To hail his returning with joyance and song.
    Merrily, merrily,
    Troll we our rhyme;
    For Christmas, glad Christmas,
    With carol and chime!

Christmas is coming! What frolic and glee;
What festive achievement of high minstrelsie;

Carousings, and revels, and lays of quaint
    rhyme,
Cheer'd his advent far back in the good
    olden time:
Through the castle's arch'd gateway proud
    cavalcades rode,
The lordly board groan'd 'neath its generous
    load,
While thronging retainers—with wassail and
    shout—
Rehearsed their bold ventures at battle and
    rout.
        Cheerily, cheerily,
        Peal'd their blithe song;
        While roof and red rafter
        The cadence prolong!

Christmas is coming!—glad news for the
    poor!
For sordid abundance will then from its store
Bring gifts to enliven the lowliest cot;
To soften the rigors of penury's lot:
Aye, blessings on Christmas! he opens the
    heart—
He bids all its kindred warm sympathies
    start

From their fast-frozen fountains, insensate
    and drear,
To gush forth in rivers of bounty and cheer.
      Merrily, merrily,
      Troll we our rhyme,
      For Christmas, glad Christmas,
      With carol and chime!

Christmas is coming! When Yule fires shall
    glow,
And parlors grow green with the mistletoe
    bough.
Around the church column, through chamber
    and hall,
Athwart the broad chimney, and over the
    wall,
Let evergreens cluster in wreath and fes-
    toon—
The work of soft fingers—a holiday boon;
Let myrtle, and holly, and noble old pine,
In leafy redundance their foliage twine.
      Daintily, daintily,
      Weave the dense screen,
      To robe merry Christmas
      In mantle of green!

Christmas is coming!—let gladness abound—
While the jest and the story go laughingly
    round;
While the table smiles gaily in opulent pride,
And bright, merry faces surround the fire-
    side;
Though long and in sadness abroad they
    may roam,
'Tis Christmas that summons the wanderers
    home;
That gilds with new lustre the family chain,
And rivets each link that was broken again.
        Merrily, merrily,
        Troll we our rhyme
        For Christmas, dear Christmas—
        With carol and chime!

FEELING.

BY J. WINANS.

"Thought is deeper than all speech;
Feeling deeper than all thought;
Soul to soul can never teach,
What unto itself is taught.—THE DIAL.

O! could we the bosom's strange secrets un-
        fold,
    And freely say all that we feel,
What a throng of emotions that may not be
        told,
    Would our tremulous accents reveal;
But feelings lie hid in the heart's secret caves,
    Too secret, too deep, to disclose,
Like gems that unseen 'neath the fathomless
        waves,
    In quiet and beauty repose.

Some trace of what passes within may appear,
    By the treacherous features confest;
A drop will gush up to the eye in a tear,
    From fountains that weep in the breast;

And from the heart's sunshine a ray often
    mounts,
  To break on the lips in a smile,
But the warm of that sunshine, the depth of
    those founts,
  Are searchless as springs of the Nile.

The glittering cavern though gorgeous and
    vast,
  (Its mouth by wild thickets o'ergrown,)
From the stroller who brushes unconciously
    past,
  Keeps all its bright secrets unknown;
Even so at the door of the spirit's deep cell,
  Some loiterer thoughtlessly treads,
Nor dreams of the glorious wonders that
    dwell
  Behind its dark rampart of weeds!

Full many a word from the lips we love
    much,
  (Though no trace of emotion be shown,)
Strikes a chord in the bosom that thrills to
    the touch,
  With an exquisite deepness of tone.

8

The heart is a harp of such delicate mould,
  No mortal can master its strings;
Awhile it breathes music impassioned and
    bold,
  Then tuneless discordantly rings.

The deer that is wounded forsakes the dense
    herd,
  In secret to suffer and moan—
And the spirit withdraws, when its sorrows
    are stirred,
  To bleed o'er the anguish alone;
But O! could we speak to some genial heart,
  And share with another our grief,
What sweet consolations might friendship
    impart,
  To give the sad spirit relief.

Alas! must it ever be counted a sin,
  Our innermost thought to unveil?
Must the vehement feelings that struggle
    within,
  Apart from all sympathy dwell?

Unseen and in silence the passion stream
flows,
Whose tides the full bosom employ—
Never sounds in its surges our wildering
woes,
Nor lisps in its ripples our joy.

TO LILLIE.

BY J. WINANS.

Deep in my bosom a secret doth dwell,
  Prison'd as closely as secret can be,
Fluttering, chafing within its lone cell;—
    O, how it longs to be free!
      Nobody knows it;
      I'll not disclose it;
  No, maid, I cannot, not even to thee!

If it could 'scape, it would hie to thine ear,
  Swiftly as hieth the dove to her nest,
Timidly whisper its fond burthen there,
    And crave a home in thy breast:
      Nobody knows it;
      I'll not expose it,
  Though it disturbs me with ceaseless un-
    rest!

Could I but utter one tremulous word,
  Fragrant with eloquent meaning for thee,
Then from its gloomy cell, like a freed bird,
  This weary captive would flee;

Nobody knows it,
I'll not disclose it;
Maiden of beauty, not even to thee!

There in its prison it sorrows and sighs,
   Till by its plainings my spirit is wrung;
There must it bide till it withers and dies,—
   Dies unreveal'd and unsung!
      Nobody knows it;
      I'll not expose it,
   To the rude breath of the slanderous
      tongue!

THE SILENT WARRIORS.

BY HERBERT C. DORR.

The sun shone in at the window,
　　On the printer's case and type,
And the heaps of mystic letters
　　Were bathed in its golden light;
And I thought of the truths there hidden,
　　Of the mighty power there laid,
In those piles of dusky metal,
　　When in marshal'd ranks arrayed.

For by them our souls find voices
　　For truths the ages have taught,
In volumes the dead have treasured,
　　In words of immortal thought;
And they have tongues for our sorrows,
　　And songs for our joys or woe,
And in them life's records are written,
　　Of all that we mortals know.

As the knights, who clad in their armor
　　Went forth in the olden days,
To war 'mid the down-trod nations,
　　With wrongs that stood in their ways,

Thus our thoughts in this dusky metal,
  Are clad in their coats of mail,
To conquer the wrongs that oppress us,
  Or evils our follies entail.

The sun in its golden glory,
  Went down 'neath the rim of night,
And each leaden shape was gleaming
  In flames of its dying light;
Then stars in their hosts came marching,
  And their silver lances fell,
And flashed on the dull, cold metal,
  Where truths we know not dwell.

A child in his feeble wisdom,
  Might place them with tiny hand,
But a king with his steel-armed legions,
  In vain would their force withstand;
For they are the silent warriors,
  Whose tents are folded away,
Whose footprints go down thro' the ages,
  Whose mandates the world shall obey.

And a thought in my soul seemed striving,
  As our own good angel strives,
To warm the clay that enfolds us,
  And wake from our sluggish lives;

That we, too, are symbols waiting
    The touch of the Master's hand,
When the truths that sleep within us
    May light up each darkened land;
And each soul on its earthly journey
    May toil with a hope sublime,
To leave for the unborn nations
    Great thoughts on the scroll of time.

A MID-SUMMER NIGHT.

BY HERBERT C. DORR.

'Tis summer's night, and Earth a bride is
  dressed,
  With silver lamps hung round her azure
  walls ;
And where Day's rosy footsteps late had
  pressed,
  The purple drapery of the evening falls.

The air is sensuous with the breath of flowers,
  Whose parted lips are drunken with de-
  light;
And on the pathways of the languid hours
  Come thousand whisper'd mysteries of the
  night.

The winds are resting in their hidden deep,
  Or coyly hide within the trembling leaves,
Where dreaming swallows twitter in their
  sleep,
  In airy nests beneath the frowning eaves.

8*

Down by the margin of the throbbing sea,
  The silent tide comes creeping on the land,
Save where, o'er rocks, it rippling glides away
  In gurgling murmurs on the yellow sand.

Along the currents of the sultry air,
    With drowsy tongue, Time counts his
      ceaseless flight;
And slumber spreads her robes o'er joys and
      care,
    While souls like sea-birds fold their wings
      in night.

Within the calm repose and dreamy hours,
    Ecstatic peace around my life is thrown;
And 'mid the fragrance of the drooping flow-
      ers,
    Soft lips like rose-buds seem to press my
      own.

Ana now the moon rolls up with ruddy glow,
    And tips with silver each far shadowy hill;
The starry hosts march onward dim and slow,
    While Nature sleeps, and Earth grows lone
      and still.

Night lies recumbent on the breast of space,
  And folds the worlds around with brood-
      ing wings ;
The Earth in moonbeams veils her dusky
      face,
  Where tranquil rest pervades all living
      things.

WHEREFORE?

BY HERBERT C. DORR.

IN hundreds and by thousands o'er the earth,
Great wondrous problems daily have their
    birth ;
They throb to live, yet wherefore?   Who
    knows why?
Or yet the wherefore they should throb to
    die?
Within each one a mystic secret lives,
And known alone to Him—the God who
    gives.
Thus through the world in fleshy robe and
    mask,
Each toiling heart pursues its fated task,
Its secret all concealed mid joy and tears,
Till trembling onward 'neath a weight of
    years,
It quivering sinks within the great unknown,
Its robe and mask in dust aside are thrown.
O heart! O life! what voice shall ever tell
The unknown wonders 'neath your mask may
    dwell ?

THE MINER'S LOT.

BY J. J. OWEN.

WHERE the snow-covered mountains un-
  fold
  Their crests, like the foam on the
    wave,—
By the rivers and streams, in their struggle
  for gold,
How many a form has gone down to the
  mold,
  The mildew and blight of the grave.

One came when the summer was young,
  And erected his cabin hard by;
No accents of mirth ever fell from his tongue,
But o'er his lone pathway the dark shadows
  hung,
  For he knew that death's portal was nigh.

We missed him one day from the spot
  Where long he had labored in vain;

With chance and misfortune he struggled and
        fought,
Till the life-spring was broken—so hard was
        lot ;—
    He never will labor again.

* * * * * * *

.

    The Yuba flows red evermore,
        As if dyed with the life-blood of toil,
And the sunset so golden with beauty gilds
        o'er
The mountain that casts its dark shade by
        his door
        Whose spirit would break from its coil.

    No woman is there with her tears,
        Or hand's gentle pressure to chide
The pain that leaps up through his temples,
        or fears
That cluster around his lone heart, as appears
        The shadowy form by his side.

    In the frenzy of fever he pines,
        And his wandering thoughts swiftly stray

To a little white cottage with clambering vines,
Now dearer by far than the wealth of the
    mines,
  · O'er mountain and valley away.

He hears the soft voice of the stream
    That trills its low notes by his door;
And the music of birds, with the sun's rosy
    beams,
Now melts all his soul into ravishing dreams,
    Like the bliss that entranced him of
    yore.

"Zalina, dear queen of my heart,
    Let me breathe out my life on thy
    breast;
Forgive the false pride that has kept us apart,
And rankled so long in my desolate heart,
    With its passions in stormy unrest.

"Forget all the years that have flown,
    With their billows of anger between;
Oh, have I not suffered enough to atone
For the pangs I have caused thee, Zalina,
    my own?—
    Let distance no more intervene."

And a voice, pure and sweet in its flow,
    As the star's silv'ry music above,
Glides over his senses, in accents so low,
Transfusing his face with a heavenly glow,—
    'Tis the soul's echoed whisper of love.
    *   *   *   *   *   *   *

By Yuba's red waters he sleeps,—
    The wind's hollow wail is his dirge—
And the dew, gentle mourner, comes nightly
    and weeps
By his grave, while the mountain its silent
    watch keeps,
    But his spirit is safe o'er the surge.

TO THE SIERRAS.

BY J. J. OWEN.

Ye snow-capped mountains, basking in the
    sun,
  Like fleecy clouds that deck the summer
    skies,
On you I gaze, when day's dull task is
    done,
  Till night shuts out your glories from my
    eyes.

For stormy turmoil, and ambition's strife,
  I find in you a solace and a balm,—
Derive a higher purpose, truer life,
  From your pale splendor, passionless and
    calm.

Mellowed by distance, all your rugged cliffs,
  And deep ravines, in graceful outlines lie;
Each giant form in silent grandeur lifts
  Its hoary summit to the evening sky.

I reck not of the wealth untold, concealed
  Beneath your glorious coronal of snows,
Whose budding treasure yet but scarce re-
    vealed,
  Shall blossom into trade—a golden rose.

A mighty realm is waking at your feet
  To life and beauty, from the lap of Time,
With cities vast, where millions yet shall
    meet,
  And Peace shall reign in majesty sublime.

Rock-ribbed Sierras, with your crests of snow,
  A type of manhood, ever strong and true,
Whose heart with golden wealth should ever
    glow,
  Whose thoughts in purity should symbol
    you.

THE VEGETABLE GIRL.

BY WURT TAYLOR.

BEHIND a market stall, installed,
  I mark it every day,
Stands at her stand the fairest girl
  I've met with at the Bay;
Her two lips are of cherry red,
  Her hands a pretty pair,
With such a pretty turn up nose,
  And lovely reddish hair.

And there she stands from morn till night,
  Her customers to please,
And to appease her appetite,
  She sells them beans and peas.
Attracted by the glances from
  The apple of her eye,
And by her Chili apples, too,
  Each passer-by will buy.

She stands upon her little feet
  Throughout the livelong day,
And sells her celery and things,
  A big feat by the way.

She changes off her stock for change,
　　Attending to each call,
And when she has but one beet left,
　　She says, "Now that beats all!"

SOMETHING TO LOVE.

BY WM. BANSMAN.

THERE are beautiful thoughts in the day-
dreams of life,
When youth and ambition join hands for the
strife;
There are joys for the gay, which come
crowding apace,
And hang out the rainbow of hope for the
race;
There are prizes to gain, which ascend as we
climb,
But the struggle to win them makes effort
sublime.
Each cloud that arises has fingers of gold,
Inviting the timid and nerving the bold;
Each sorrow is tempered with something of
sweet,
And the crag, while it frowns, shows a niche
for the feet.
There are charms in the verdure which na-
ture has spread,
And the sky shows a glory of stars overhead,

And the zephrys of summer have voices to
    woo,
As well as to bear the perfumes from the
    dew;
There are gushes of transport in dreams of
    the night,
When memory garners its thoughts of de-
    light,
And the soul seeks its kindred, and noise-
    lessly speaks,
In the smiles and the blushes of health-
    blooming cheeks.
There are rapturous melodies filling the
    heart,
With emotions which nothing beside could
    impart;
And yet, though this cumulous picture may
    show
The brightest of joys which ambition would
    know—
Though the heaven it opens is one of sur-
    prise,
All gorgeous with hope, and prismatic with
    dyes,

Satiety follows these transports of bliss,
And the heart asks a lodgment more real
        than this;
Like the dove, it will wander, and still, like
        the dove,
Come back, till it rests upon something to
        love.

SIR JOHN FRANKLIN.

BY W. F. STEWART.

OLD Sir John was a mariner bold
  As ever laid hand to helm;
Nor reck'd he aught of hunger or cold,
Nor trembled he when the black waves roll'd
  In hyperborean realm.

Away, away to the frozen zone
  The gallant Sir John did go;
But mad Eolus, with angry groan,
Muttering many a midnight moan,
  Mock'd at the mariner's woe.

Then spoke the shivering Esquimaux,
  On his desolate ice-girt rock:
"What doth the pale-face seek to know,
Here in the realm of eternal snow,
  By lonely Anoatok?

"Why doth the white man dare to brave
  The storms of Anoatok?

Why, why hath he left the tepid wave
To lay his bones in a frozen grave
  By the beetling, wind-loved rock?

"Go, white man, go, while the sun doth
    glow,
  Nor dare the terrible gloom,
For soon the shimmering ice will flow,
And the long, long night with its pall of
    snow
  Will thee and thy ship entomb."

But old Sir John was a sailor bold
  As ever laid hand to helm;
Nor reck'd he aught of danger or cold,
Nor trembled he when the black waves roll'd
  In hyperborean realm.

He only laughed at the warning giv'n
  By the shivering Esquimaux,
And boldly shouted, as northward driv'n,
"I'll lift the pole-star higher in heav'n,
  And earth's dark mystery know."

Away, away did the good ship fly
  By many a dreary coast;

9

But Boreas chased the sun from the sky,
And hung a pall o'er the stars on high,
   And gallant Sir John was lost.

The hungry bear, from his snowy lair
   On a dismal Greenland rock,
Doth greedily snuff the frozen air,
For mariner's bones are dainty fare
   For the beasts of Anoatok.

IN THE MINES.

BY JOHN SWETT.

Leave the sluice and "tom" untended,
　Shadows darken on the river;
In the canon day is ended,
　Far above the red rays quiver;
Lay aside the bar and spade,
　Let the pick-axe cease from "drifting,"
See how much the claim has paid
　Where the gold dust has been sifting.

Tell no tales of wizard charm,
　In the myths of ages olden,
When the sorcerer's potent arm
　Turned all earthly things to golden;—
Pick and spade are magic rods
　In the brawny hands of miners;
Mightier than the ancient gods,
　Laboring men are true diviners.

Gather round the blazing fire
　In the deepening darkness gleaming,
While the red tongues leaping higher
　Seem like banners upward streaming;

Stretched around the fiery coals,
　　Lulled into luxurious dreaming,
Half-a-dozen hungry souls
　　Watch the iron kettle steaming.

Break the bread with ready hand,
　　Labor crowns it with a blessing,—
Now the hungry crowd looks bland,
　　Each a smoking piece possessing;
Pass the ham along this way,
　　Quick! before the whole is taken;
Hang philosophy, we say,
　　If we only save our bacon!

Spread the blankets on the ground,
　　We must toil again to-morrow;
Labor brings us slumber sound
　　No luxurious couch can borrow;
Watch the stars drift up the sky,
　　Bending softly down above us,
Till in dreams our spirits fly
　　Homeward to the friends who love us.

As the needle, frail and shivering,
　　On the ocean wastes afar,
Veering, changing, trembling, quivering,
　　Settles on the polar star;

So in souls of those who roam,
Love's magnetic fires are burning,
To the loved ones left at home
Throbbing hearts are ever turning.

SONG OF LABOR; THE MINER.

BY JOHN SWETT.

The eastern sky is blushing red,
  The distant hill-top glowing;
The brook is murmuring in its bed,
  In idle frolics flowing;
'Tis time the pickaxe and the spade,
  And iron "tom" were ringing,
And with ourselves, the mountain stream,
  A song of labor singing.

The mountain air is cool and fresh,
  Unclouded skies bend o'er us,
Broad placers, rich in hidden gold,
  Lie temptingly before us;
We ask no magic Midas' wand,
  Nor wizard-rod divining,
The pickaxe, spade and brawny hand
  Are sorcerers in mining.

When labor closes with the day,
  To simple fare returning,
We gather in a merry group
  Around the camp-fires burning;

The mountain sod our couch at night,
　The stars shine bright above us,
We think of home and fall asleep,
　To dream of those who love us.

DIED ON THE BATTLE-FIELD.

BY WILLIAM WAIFE.

THE summer sun was setting o'er the green
    Virginia plains,
Slowly creep the lengthening shadows,—into
    night the evening wanes;
And his last beams rested sadly on the dying
    and the dead,
On the groaning and the wounded, with which
    the field was spread.
Low amidst them lay a soldier from the far-
    off Quaker State,
With a crimson streamlet oozing slow beneath
    his cross-belt plate;
And a bronzed, rough face bent o'er him as
    his clammy hand he press'd,
To catch the faltering words which came in
    gaspings from his breast.

"I'm dying, comrade; raise my head, my eyes
    are growing dim,
A strange and numbing coldness is creeping
    o'er each limb,—

The pain is quite gone from my side, the
    blood has ceased to flow,
But I want to tell you something, comrade,
    ere to my rest I go.
I've been praying as I lay here—and I think
    that God will hear—
For those to whom I'd have you go when I'm
    no longer near,
Pardon for all my many sins, and strength
    for those at home;
Oh, tell them how I thought of them when
    dying here alone.

"Oh, mother, mother,—would to God I
    might have died near you,
Your gentle hand to touch my face, your eyes
    to look into,
Don't forget me, darling mother, don't for-
    get your wandering son,
But think I died in battle, when the bloody
    fight was done.
And tell her, comrade, that I thought of what
    she said to me,
When she kissed the last good-by, beneath
    the old oak tree,—

9*

When she bid me fight as father fought, if at
    my post I fell,—
And when the fight was raging hot, I kept
    my promise well !

"And my little sister—tell her that I wore
    the sash she made,
That 'twas strongly knit, and more than that,
    the color did not fade;
She said she thought it would, but, alas, my
    life has faded first ;
And take the sash back to her,—give me
    water, Tom, I thirst.
Poor Louise ! she will take it hardly to lose
    her brother Will,
For I used to play along with her, upon the
    pleasant hill ;
But tell her that I thought of her when my
    life was ebbing low,
And bid you kiss her for me,—for she's only
    twelve, you know.

"Tell my brother Alfred that I wished I had
    him here with me,
That we might have battled side by side in
    combat for the free ;

But that he must stay with mother now that
    I have passed away,
And comfort her and sister—tell him be sure
    to stay ;
And bid him sometimes think of me and of
    the days gone by,
When together we went fishing in the still
    Neshammy;
And that his dying brother prayed to God
    that he would bless
And keep him, as He's promised e'er to keep
    the fatherless.

"Oh, comrade, bend down lower,—my
    strength is going fast,
I've only one more message— tis the bitter-
    est and the last.
There's a blue-eyed girl in waiting, far away,
    for my return,—
Oh, God, whene'er I think of her my brain
    begins to burn!
When I've been on picket all alone, in the
    rainy, stormy night,
When I've led the men to battle in the wild
    and desperate fight,

When I've laid me down at night upon the
    wet and cheerless ground,
Her face has always hovered near—the only
    joy I found.

"Take her this locket from my side, close
    where the red blood drips,
And tell her that I died with her sweet name
    upon my lips.
She put the locket round my neck, when by
    my side she sat,—
There's a spot of blood upon it, but perhaps
    she'll like it more for that.
Oh, darling, darling Nettie, 'tis bitter thus
    to die,
I could have died right gladly had only you
    been by,
For I loved you better, better far than life, or
    aught men love,—
But I'll see you sometime, darling Net, in
    the better land above.

"And tell her,"—but his voice grew hushed,
    his fading eye grew dim,
A sudden tremor shook his frame,—then
    ceased—and all was still.

His chilly hand dropped down like lead, as
    his comrade lower bent,—
His gallant soul had passed away, his brave
    young life was spent.
And a blue-eyed girl was praying on a Penn-
    sylvania farm,
That God would bless her soldier boy, and
    keep him safe from harm.
But as she prayed, a weary spirit floated up
    to God,
And a silent form lay motionless on the torn
    and bloody sod.

PHILOMEL.

BY ISAAC H. STEWART.

O, THE lovely Philomel !
Tell me, where do fairies dwell?
In a bower of silken roof
Of sunbeam warp and gossamer woof;
There, 'mong fairy folks, should dwell
The lovely, lovely Philomel.

O, the glance of Philomel !
Soft blue eyes, that laughing say
" Remember me, remember May,
Remember skies of softest blue,
Remember violets wet with dew,
Remember still the sweet blue bell,
And think on love, and Philomel."

O, the smile of Philomel !
Holds my heart the picture there?
Guard it then as jewel rare;
Simile can never tell
The rapturous smile of Philomel.

O, the laugh of Philomel
Think upon a mossy dell
With a stream that limps along,
Humming to the linnet's song;
Like sweetest chime of sabbath bell
Peals the laugh of Philomel.

O, the face of Philomel!
Is there such another face?
Could the hand of artist trace
Lines of beauty fit to spell
The classic face of Philomel?

O, the grace of Philomel!
All the Graces who have strayed
Where poets painted Phidian maid—
Blooming Venus in her shell,
Pales to lovely Philomel.

O, the hair of Philomel!
'Prisoned not in vulgar cage,
By contortion's wayward rage—
Free as fancy's joyful swell,
Flow the curls of Philomel.

O, the form of Philomel!
Who upon that form could gaze
And not feel his heart a-blaze?
Little Cupid, you should sell
Your bow and shafts to Philomel.

O, the blush of Philomel!
'Tis a tint of heaven's dye—
Lightning of an angel's sigh,
Who grieves, from heaven aught should
      dwell
So pure as lovely Philomel.

O, the love of Philomel!
Deep and rich as diamond mine,
Buried in her heart doth shine;
O, that some sweet fairy spells
Would mingle mine with Philomel's!

LEARN TO SWEEP.

BY H. S. BROOKS.

ONCE, in a city's crowded street,
With broom in hand, an urchin stood;
No boots inclosed the little feet,
Tho' winter chilled the infant blood;
And yet he worked, the little man
As only youthful heroes can,
And as he toiled he cheerful sang:
"The noblest oak was once a seed,
The choicest flower was but a weed,
Unpinioned once the eaglet's wing,
The river but a trickling spring, .
The swiftest foot must learn to creep,
The proudest man must learn to sweep."

Anon some passing idlers sought
The sweeper from his toil to shame,
To scorn the noble worker's thought,
And quench the young aspiring flame;
No answer gave the hero back,
But to and fro he whisked the broom,
And shouted as he cleared the track:

"The noblest oak was once a seed,
The choicest flower was but a weed,
Unpinioned once the eaglet's wing,
The river but a trickling spring,
The swiftest foot must learn to creep,
The proudest man must learn to sweep."

A REVERIE.

BY WASHINGTON AYER, M. D.

When starry light the azure fills
  With voiceless melody,
And moonbeams melt upon the hills,
  And quiver on the sea,

Alone I tread the busy streets,
  Unmindful where I be,
As then my heart in sadness beats,
  Life seems so strange to me.

And yet some weird emotion thrills
  The heart once full of glee,
And leads me far o'er slumbering hills,
  Beyond bright lakes and sea.

And there the sportive scenes of youth—
  Those spectres of the past,
Come dancing 'round my path forsooth,
  In fleecy shadows cast;—

And lead me where the fern is gray,
  Through pastures bright and green,
Where violets along the way
  And buttercups are seen.

Again o'er dimpled hills I stray,
  Along the shady mead,
And chase the butterfly away,
  Upon my willow steed.

But oh! what dreamy spell is this?
  What wandering of the mind?
My early sports and youthful bliss
  Leave but this dream behind.

Then up! by daily toil beguiled!
  Nor slumber by the stream,
Where phantoms lead the simple child
  In innocence to dream.

Life is at best a lingering death,—
  A journey not of miles,—
And hope, the only rainbow wreath,
  Is wrought of tears and smiles.

The labor of the fleeting years
  Is all we have to give;
Then up! and drive away the tears,
  And dying, learn to live!

JENNY WADE.

ANONYMOUS.

THE Nation's love has honored well
The heroes who at Gettysburg fell.

No orator or poet's line
Has praised a single heroine.

Yet on that ground is not a grave
That holds a heart more true and brave

Than that where tenderly was laid
The form of gentle Jenny Wade.

Where base invaders boldly trod,
In pride, on loyal Northern sod,

And freemen rose to armed dispute,
And squadrons pressed in swift pursuit,

The frowning bolts of war came down
On Gettysburg's own peaceful town;

And they who dreamed of war before,
Heard trumpets sound and cannon roar,

And saw the tides of battle beat
In deadly onset and retreat.

Not many who could fly, I ween,
Remained to view the dreadful scene.

But one undaunted, gentle heart
Disdained the warning to depart.

There, in the thickest counter-fire,
Where battle raged with deadliest ire,

The danger viewing undismayed,
Stood at her post brave Jenny Wade.

Her's were the maiden's bloom and years,
Her's were the maiden's hopes and fears,

But her's the love and loyalty
That dared to suffer and to die.

"Our soldiers are in need of bread;
I'll stay and bake it here," she said.

Many a hungry friend and foe
Stifled his pangs and bade her go.

Thousands, to see the maid secure,
Had abjured food for evermore.

Heedless of every warning breath,
Heedless of danger and of death,

Staunch in duty, the brave heart stood,
Till the foeman's fire shed its blood.

Where Gettysburg's heroes have been laid,
Brave as the bravest, sleeps Jenny Wade.

The years shall come in endless pursuit,
With returning verdure, bloom and fruit;

And the birds, as the seasons rise and decline,
Make their pilgrimages from the Palm to
    the Pine;

But the foe who came when the summer's
    store
Was rich in the fields, shall come no more.

And a Nation shall sing: O, not in vain,
Were they who sleep at Gettysburg slain!

They were the steadfast breasts that withstood
The shock of the fierce, invading flood;

They were the the heroes true and great,
Who dashed back the waves from the ship
    of State.

And she, embalmed in her country's tears,
She of the maiden bloom and years,

Though her gentle hand could wield no
    sword
To repel the march of the rebel horde,

In purpose as firm, in duty as brave,
Was great as the greatest who died to save.

For a maiden's love and a maiden's prayer,
Give strength to the hero's arm in war;

And the will of a maid who dares to bleed,
Is good and great as the warrior's deed.

Freedom shall mourn where her dead are
    laid,
No champion truer than Jenny Wade.

PICTURES IN SILVER-LAND.

BY E. P. HINGSTON.

COME to me, from shores Atlantic, letter in a
    loved one's hand,
Saying, "Paint me in your word-lore, pic-
    tures of the Silver-land,
Paint me Washoe, as you see it, tinting with
    a truthful touch;
Limn it with a faithful pencil; do not color
    overmuch."
While the coach climbs up the summit, read-
    ing o'er the dear request,
Out of love and out of duty, I obey my
    love's behest.
Sketch-book ready, eyes wide open, pencil
    steady in my hand—
Here are sketches, here are pictures taken in
    the Silver-land.

Foreground—the snow-white Sierra. Morn-
    ing breaks o'er distant scene,
Lake Tahoe is gleaming brightly, all the
    rocky world between,

10

Height six thousand feet or higher on the
    summit of the pass,
Zig-zag grades in constant curvings glitt'ring
    with icy glass,
Coaches gliding down the snow-way—sliding
    on a mountain shelf—
Slipp'ry is the path men travel, when in haste
    they seek for pelf.
On my left a wall of granite—on my right a
    chasm deep,
Where, in man-untrodden ravines Nature
    sleeps her virgin sleep.
Snow and pine trees—pines and snow-drift;
    mountain peaks and glaciers high,
Solemn grandeur, awful stillness—purest air
    and cloudless sky,
Beauteous Tahoe, clear and lucid, glassing its
    mirror bright,
Every craggy peak around it golden in the
    morning light.
Fairest lake of crystal splendor! Blending
    in its holy calm
Leman's quiet, placid beauty, and Lake
    Thun's romantic charm,

Luring on the silver-seeker with its fascina-
    tion bland—
Beauty leads the way to labor!—*Picture one
    of Silver-land.*

Foreground now, the Second Summit. Snow-
    clad mountains round me rise,
Amphitheatre majestic!—God's own rearing
    to the skies.
Deep, down deep mine eyes are peering till
    my senses dizzy grow,
Down the frightful precipices to the gloomy
    depths below.
Round the hollow of the mountains, winds
    with serpent twist and twirl,
Granite-hewn, the graded roadway, down
    which at mad pace we whirl.
Coaches, clinging, hanging, dangling to the
    rugged mountain side;
Wagons playing flies and spiders 'gainst the
    rock-wall as they slide.
Far away a scene discloses—strangely solemn
    —wildly strange!
Lay aside all brilliant colors. Painter now
    the pallett change,

Bring me umber, bring me sepias, Vandyke,
    and all tints of brown,
Whatsoe'er will best paint Nature where she
    wears her gloomiest frown.
Like a ruined world it seemeth—burnt, up-
    turned and scarred by fire,
Vestige of Almighty vengeance—record of
    Almighty ire!
Mountains in amorphous masses—sea-beds
    of some earlier sea;
Land whereon no flower bloometh—never
    grows umbrageous tree,
Dreary hills and drearier valleys—howling
    wastes of sage-clad sand—
Chaos of God's first creation!—*Picture two
in Silver-land.*

Once an outpost, now a city, this is Carson,
    fairly drawn,
As I sketch it, roughly tinted, on this bright
    December morn,
Crater of some dead volcano—lava bed of
    later lake;
Says the pioneer, staunch-hearted, "Here
    will I a city make!"

Lay it out in quadrilaterals. This a plaza,
    that a street,
Stores of granite, wooden shanties, cottages
    with gardens neat.
Here the soil, with careful tillage, yields its
    luscious crops of corn,
Concentrating here its verdure in a wilderness
    forlorn.
Circling round me, rise the mountains; arid
    hills the place invest,
Save where pines and crags commingle—look-
    ing backwards to the west.
One long row of streets and bar-rooms rang-
    ed upon the western side ;
Eastward, views of plains of sage brush,
    where the vista opens wide.
Busy throngs of motley people—pioneers of
    every race,
Eastern, Western, Jew and Gentile, Chinese,
    Negro, Indian face,
Traders with thin-visaged aspects, hunters
    with their nets and guns,
Speculators, politicians, Labor's horny-fisted
    sons,

Building up the nascent city of the great State
 yet to be,
Waking in the waste—a desert—all the
 sounds of energy,
Bearing with the Cyclop's power, traffic's
 . marts and happy homes,
Legislative halls and chambers, temples, towers, spires and domes.
Such the ground-plot, such the future, roughly sketched, but grandly planned,
Of this strange young Carson city!—*Picture
 three in Silver-land.*

PERISHED RACES.

BY REV. J. D. STRONG.

In a deep, dank glen, where the smiling sun
Never kissed the tears from the weeping noon,
'Mid the graves of a race that have passed
    away,
Where dim aisles lead and dark shadows play,
With the sounds of a rill that goes singing
    by,
May be heard deep tones, like a spirit's sigh:
    "Doomed!   Doomed!
    Our race is spent,
    Will none lament?"

When the morning breaks from the clasp of
    night,
And the anthem of birds greets the growing
    light;
When the burning sun, with a fierce, bold
    ray,
Drives the quail and the deer from the glade
    away;

When the night woos stars to its fond em-
    brace,
Then the voice floats up from the depths of
    space:
        "Doomed! Doomed!
        Must pity sleep?
        Will no eye weep?"

When tne spring's soft breath, in the fragrant
    May,
Warms the buds into life, where the young
    leaves play;
When the autumn air, with a frosty frown,
Clothes the hills and the glades in a russet
    brown;
When the forest wails, and the dead leaves
    moan,
Then the voice still cries, with a raven tone:
        "Doomed! Doomed!
        And never a word
        Of the wrong be heard!"

When the sun's sweet light, like the breath
    of God,
With a thousand hues bathes the springing
    sod;

Or the King of Storms, in his warrior wrath,
Treads over the fields his desolate path,
Through the old dead pines the sad wind
    sighs,
And the same weird tone forever replies:
      "Doomed! Doomed!
      But remember, God
      Still holds the rod!"

10*

GRADING THE STREET.

BY MISTUR MALOONY.

'Twas miself thin as bot me a swate little lot,
Wid monies I digged for six years in the
mines;
An' I builded an' plastered a duck o' a cot,
Which Biddy soon kivird wid crapers and
vines,
Wid a back-yard and garding convanyent
and neat,
Where the childer and pig could kape out o'
the street.

I warked wid the hod an' had plinty to do,
An' a stitch in my back ne'er minded at all;
Our childer was healthy and Biddy was true,
And I sung 'neath the load as I mounted the
wall.
For I knew when at sundown my work was
complete,
My supper was ready, all smoking and sweet.

'Twas down in a valley secure from the wind,
A sand-hill a north and a sand-hill a south ;
I thought that dame nature to me was so
    kind
She had opened her jaws an' we lived in her
    mouth.
Biddy oft at the sand would objection and
    grete,
But I tould her 'twould stop whin they
    graded the street.

Bad luck to the day thin—one Saturday night
I came back from working two month and
    a week ;
Och! sorry an inch o' my cot was in sight,
'T was kivered wid sand an' all livil and sleek ;
I thought that an earthquake had made the
    hills meet,
Till poor Biddy cried out, "They've graded
    the street !"

"Bad luck to their sowls, thin," I cried in
    my hate;
"I'll sue them for spoiling my cottage an'
    land,"
Whin Biddy sobbed out, "Dear Pat, ye are
    late,

'Tis a bill agin us that I hould in my hand,"
In trouble I looked at the figgirs complete,
And saw *"four hundred dollars"* for grading
    the street!

Poor Biddy was faithful, an' didn't repine ;
Her cousin the childer an' her had took in,
'Till I could wid our laving another house
    find;
Wid a few pots an' kettles a new life begin;
But exparience had taught me a lesson I weet,
Ne'er to live in a valley beside o' the street.

So I wint to the highest o' hills I could find,
An' rinted a place that commanded a view,
An' got oursilves sittled so much to our
    mind,
I soon earned the monies, an' paid for it, too;
'Twas not so convanyent, but still it was
    neat,
Tho' my bones ached at night, as I toiled up
    the street.

The young uns grew healthy, the air was so
    good,
An' Biddy her clothes dried in half o' the
    time ;

Fur to help me to pay fur our vittals an' food,
The poor girl by washing earned many a
dime,
An' she kept things so tidy, complaicint an'
sweet,
I nivir grudgid climin' that hill o' a street.

Thin I wint to the mines for six month it may
be, ·
An' wid goold in my pockit I hurried me
back;
Whin I got to the hill, nary hill could I see;
'T was gone, an' some lumber obstructed my
track—
I saw in an instant my ruin complete—
Och! faith and Saint Peter, *they'd graded the
street!*

THE SPIRIT LOVER.

BY J. H. ROGERS.

He comes in the night,
Like a pure soft light,
And hovers around me while sleeping;
Though my eyelids may close
In their earthly repose,
My soul knows the watch he is keeping.

From the pure azure skies,
When the sunbeams arise,
I see his bright spirit descending;
In my garden of flowers,
He will linger for hours,
His life, with their loveliness blending.

His soul comes to me,
On life's troubled sea,
When passion waves roll in their madness;
I see through the storm
His bright spirit form
Fold my soul to his own in its sadness.

Through the smiles and tears
Of fast-flitting years,
His spirit around me will hover;
When earth life is o'er
On the bright golden shore,
I shall stand with my own spirit lover.

ROSALIE.

BY B. F. WASHINGTON.

Now twilight sits upon the hills,
And lengthened shades the valley fill;
The wild bird's song is hushed, and still
  Is dreaming nature, Rosalie;
While here within this spot, o'ergrown
With leaves and flowers, I sit alone,
To muse on thee and hours flown,
  Love-winged and joyous, Rosalie.

To muse upon those happy times,
When first I won thee with my rhymes,
When sweet as music's vesper chimes,
  Our hearts accorded, Rosalie;
When life flow'd ever like the stream
Of some brain-pictured lovely dream,
Where airy shapes and fancies gleam
  Upon its bright waves, Rosalie.

Afar in mem'ry's misty light—
As stars steal through the gloom of night—
The twinklings of a vision bright
  Come gently o'er me, Rosalie;

A vine-clad cot beneath the hill—
The gladsome wanderings of a rill—
A form which love's bright beamings fill—
    Are all before me, Rosalie.

Once more we walk this wildwood shade,
Where oft in 'love's young dream' we stray'd;
Again upon the flowery glade
    We pluck bright blossoms, Rosalie;
Once more I hear the wild bird's song
That charmed us all the summer long,
And with it comes a glorious throng
    Of bright-winged visions, Rosalie.

And as the stars come out to-night,
All trembling on their lonely height,
Methinks amid their dewey light
    Thine eyes shine on me, Rosalie;
Those soft, those gently-speaking eyes,
Where hopes and pleasant memories,
Like silver waves, alternate rise
    Upon a bright sea, Rosalie.

Thy face to me was as a tide,
Where barks, love-laden, ever glide,
With Hope, their pilot and their guide,
    And I their haven, Rosalie;

But ah! a cloud on swift wings passed,
And all the sky was overcast,
And then were wrecked, alas! too fast,
     My freighted treasures, Rosalie.

I can not twine my fingers now
In thy soft hair, nor kiss thy brow,
Nor hear thy gentle accents flow
     In murmur'd music, Rosalie;
I can not feel thy breath so warm
Upon my cheek, nor press thy form,
Which, like a flow'ret in a storm,
     Slept on my bosom, Rosalie.

And tho' each wild bird sings of thee,
And in each summer flower I see
Thy own eyes, bright exceedingly,
     Look up and greet me, Rosalie;
I start and sigh to think that thou
Art but, to me, a mem'ry now—
A star that gemmed life's morning brow,
     Then fled and left me, Rosalie.

A tall oak stricken in its pride—
The fierce red bolt has rent its side—
Scatters its sear'd leaves far and wide
     Upon the cold heath, Rosalie;

So too my heart is sorely riven .
By a stern fate, 'gainst which I've striven,
Till my poor thoughts like leaves are driven
    Upon a rude world, Rosalie.

And I have sought to find, in vain
This vision of my youth again;
And I have dream'd until my brain
    Was wild with dreaming, Rosalie;
But oh! to sit and muse alone,
Within this spot with flowers o'ergrown,
Is all that's left me now, my own,
    My lost, my lovely Rosalie.

MORNING IN THE MOUNTAINS.*

BY B. F. WASHINGTON.

THE morning is up and the earth is all glee,
Her glories are gleaming from rock and from
tree,
And my steps are away to the wild mountain
side,
Where tower the fir and the pine in their
pride.

Look afar and around, where so barren and
bleak,
In an endless succession of peak after peak,
The hoar mountains rise, with their feet
clothed in green,
While snowy white wreaths on their summits
are seen.

Those nearest are bright with the rose-tints
of morn—
Those farthest, thin blue mist of beauty
adorn,

*These lines were written on the Trinity Mountains, California.

And every gradation of color is seen
To linger and play on the bald peaks be-·
    tween.

How lovely the scene thus spread out to the
    eye—
The glories of earth and the· glories of sky
Are blended so nicely, a shade more or less
Would destroy the charm of its full perfect-
    ness.

And see now' where CLEAR CREEK comes
    bounding along,
With footstep all fleetness and voice all song,
While hither and thither so strangely she
    goes,
One scarcely knows whither her bright water
    flows.

For now she goes creeping where slopes the
    hill down,
And now wildly leaping where wildly rocks
    frown,
And now like a child all fatigued in its play,
She rests mid the flowers, then dashes away.

'Tis said that her lover is hid in these hills,
Be-sporting himself with the wild mountain
    rills,
And blinded by love and the trees on her
    banks,
She plays, in her search for him, all these
    wild pranks.

But she finds him at last in his green haunts
    away,
And, O! how she laughs as she dashes the
    spray
From her gay sunny ringlets, then joyously
    on,
They flow with their bright waves all mingled
    in one.

But mark now that fine bird high-poised in
    the air—
How he watches the waters! pray what sees
    he there?
'Tis something, I'm sure, that is worth being
    seen,
His look is so anxious, his vision so keen.

With sudden quick motion and wings close
    to side,
Like an arrow he falls, and the waters divide;
For a moment now lost, but he soon re-
    appears,
And proudly his prey in his talons he bears.

Rejoice now, thou   sh-hawk! in feat so well
    done,
For bravely deserved is the prize thou hast
    won;
Yet haste, be away! for a vision as keen
As thine own, from afar, all thy movements
    has seen.

And see now, he comes! with a pinion and
    eye
Which proclaim him the monarch, fast cleav-
    ing the sky:
And O! what a rushing and flapping of
    wings,
As wild from her perch the poor fisher-bird
    springs.

Now down to the earth you can mark their
    wild flight—
Now up in the air to the limits of sight—

Now doublings full many our bold sailor
    tries,
To elude the pursuit of the king of the skies.

But fisher-bird, fisher-bird, vain is thy flight!
Thy fine trout must go as a tribute to-night,
And well for thy plumage that high in the
    air,
Thy talons unclose on the burden they bear.

And shame! on that pirate king—see how
    he springs,
With look full of triumph and downward-
    turned wings,
And seizes in mid air the fisher-bird's prey—
Then proudly he soars to his eyrie away.

Thus pleasant it is in the morning's sweet
    prime,
To lay aside care and the tall hills to climb,
And feel, though encompass'd by troubles
    below,
We here bid them thus far, and no farther go.

The mind too exults in a life more intense—
How quicken'd in thought and enliven'd the
    sense!

We feel as each moment flies hurrying on,
A gem of rare price from our pleasures has
  gone.

Then here where the mountain˙breeze makes
  of this pine,
A harp of rich melody, let me recline,
And revel the hours with nature alone,
Her works of wild beauty and dreams of my
  own.

And not till the moon with her mellowing
  beam,
Has tipt the wild forests and silver'd the
  stream,
Shall my steps all reluctant descend to the
  plain,
To mingle with men on the morrow again.

11

DAY BY DAY.

BY ELDRIDGE G. PAIGE, ("DOW, JR.")

Day by day old sorrows leave us,
   Leave us while new sorrows come;
Come, like evening's shadows, lengthening,
   Lengthening round the spirit's home.
Day by day fade friendship's flowers—
   Flowers that flourished in the past—
Past, oh, past! once bright and glowing,
   Glowing once, but dimmed at last;
Last to fade of all is fancy—
   Fancy, ever young and gay,
Gay as when young love was dreaming,
   Dreaming, dreaming, day by day.

Day by day come wondrous changes,
   Changes pluming mighty thought—
Thought that wings its way far onward,
   Onward, unto scenes unsought.
Day by day new hopes are rising,
   Rising, gilded all with bliss;
Bliss that never reaches mortals,
   Mortals in a world like this!

This vain world—how false and fleeting!
  Fleeting as the sunset's ray—
Ray that says to man, "Thou 'rt dying—
  Dying, dying, day by day.

CHILDREN.

BY J. C. DUNCAN.

PATTERING through the parlors,
  Romping overhead,
Racing in the garden,
  Tumbling in the bed;
Laughing in the morning,
  At the peep of light,
Kissing in the evening,
  When they bid "good-night;"
Tugging at my heart-strings,
  Hour, and day, and year,
Cling the little children
  God has sent me here.

Nestling thick around me
  When I seek my home,
Anxious for the greeting
  Which is *sure* to come;
Striving first to reach me,
  Trooping down the stair,
Drowning with their voices,
  Throbs of daily care;

Closing all around me,
　To keep the world away,
Lifting up the heavy years,
　Pressing day by day,
Tinting with the rainbow
　Every falling tear,
Minister the children
　God has sent me here.

Barren would this world be,
　Should these buds of life
Wither at my hearth-stone,
　Leave me in the strife,
Falling by the way-side
　Ere *my* years are done,
Darkening the sunlight
　Childhood's smile has won—
Closing up the fountain,
　Stilling laugh and shout,
Piling up the waste sands,
　Blotting my garden out;
Leaving me so weary,
　Nothing more could bring
Living thoughts to winter,
　One green leaf to spring.

Beating thus my heart clings
　Hour, and day, and year,
Closer round the children
　God has sent me here.

CHRISTMAS AT SEA.

BY J. C. DUNCAN.

THE merry noise of children's glee,
　The blazing hearth to sit before,—
Far out upon the cheerless sea,
　I dream I see the open door—
　　The open door that leads to joy;
　　The sailor's wife, the sailor's boy!

The blue waves slowly rise and fall,
　The petrel skims the darkened deep,
My heart, in unison with all,
　Wells up the tears I would not weep:
　　That cottage door is not for me,
　　It changes to the cheerless sea.

Again I see it there afar!
　Away amidst the mists of night,
Where Hope, the sailor's guiding star,
　Beams brightly as a beacon light:
　　The port once gained, the voyage past,
　　The door will open there at last!

A SONG.

BY J. C. DUNCAN.

Look upon me, ever smiling,
　　Look with love-light in thine eyes,
Look to see thy glance beguiling,
　　Look to see how sorrow flies!

Whispers to me midst the flowers,
　　Whisper words beneath the rose,
Whispering through day's sunny hours,
　　Whisper still to evening's close.

Trust me with each thought and feeling,
　　Trust me with each shade of fear,
Trust me without look appealing,
　　Trust me far, as bending near.

Love me with a gentle loving,
　　Loving as they love above,
Love without the power of roving,
　　Love with life, and life with love.

THE LONE PINE.

BY B. P. AVERY.

Sway thy top, thou ancient pine—
Warrior of the storm commading?
Lone upon the mountain standing,
Where no ivy's arms entwine.
Melancholy souls like mine,
'Neath thy shadow passing slow,
Love to hear thy plaintive moan;
'Tis an echo of the woe
Found in human breasts alone.

Mournfully amid the ruins
Of thy fellows standest thou,
Like a column of some temple
Living but in story now;
All around it wildly scattered,
Fallen walls and pillars shattered,
Softly sighing through thy branches
Sounds the wind, with fall and swell;
Now retreats, and now advances,
Rousing fancy with its spell,
Like the melody that chances
On the ear from distant bell,

Or the murmer that entrances
Of the tinted sea side shell.
Lo! musing on thy loneliness,
Thy brethren seem again to rise;
On every hand a wilderness
Shuts out the prospect of the skies.

'Tis verdure all, and deepest shade.   No
    sound
Disturbs the thoughtful silence, save
A murmur such as rolls through ocean
    cave,
A rustling of dry leaves upon the ground.
But while I listen with an awe profound,
A glance dispels the visionary wood—
A single tree remains where late ten thou-
    sand stood.

SONG OF THE MARINER'S NEEDLE

BY C. R. CLARKE.

Ho! burnish well, ye cunning hands,
   A palace-home for me,
For I would ride in royal state
   Across the briny sea.
Bring ivory from the Indian main,
   To pave my mystic floor,
And build my dome of crystal sheen,
   My walls of shining ore.

Now mount the wave, ye fearful ones,
   Though raging storms assail,
My sparry lance o'ercometh all—
   My arm is sheathed in mail.
The storm-fiend wraps his murky clouds
   Around your trembling sight,
But I can pierce that gloomy vail,
   And soar beyond the night.

The lone Enchantress of the Deep,
   I rule its boisterous realm;
Watch ye my lithe and quivering wand,
   To guide your straining helm.

Ay, bend your anxious gaze on me!
  The polar star is dim,
And waves and tempests ill the night
  With ocean's awful hymn.

For I commune with spirit-forms
  Within my wizard cell,
And brooding shadows wing their flight
  Before my magic spell.
O, angel of my constant heart,
  O, peerless northern star!
What midnight shall our spirits part—
  Our sweet communings mar!

And sapient eyes have watched me long,
  And science has grown gray,
And still ye dream not how nor why
  I keep my wondrous way.
Ye know me as ye know the storm
  That heaps your heaving path;
Ye love me, though, since mine is not
  The mystery of wrath!

THE LIFTING OF THE VAIL.

BY MRS. E. A. SIMONTON PAGE.

BETWEEN the Here and the Hereafter,
    Heaven's repose and earthly strife,
Hangs a mystic screen dividing
    Souls from souls, and life from life.
Soft as dew falls on the waters,
    Or the mist o'er mount and dale,
Soundless as a bud's unfolding
    Is the lifting of the veil.

When we pine with restless yearning,
    Some long-vanished form to view,
Seems the veil a luminous ether,
    Saintly faces smiling through.
We can almost catch their whispers,
    Sweet as sigh of summer gale—
Almost see the beckoning fingers,
    And the lifting of the veil.

Yet when all the soul is weary
    Of life's turmoil, pain and whirl,
Till we strive to rend the curtain—
    Lo! we beat but walls of pearl.

We have missed the crystal doorways,
　　Or the keys celestial fail—
And we wait without, impatient
　　For the lifting of the veil.

When a face we love grows pallid,
　　Purer, clearer, day by day,
Till we see the spirit's lustre
　　Shining through its tent of clay,
Or when the jewel leaves the casket,
　　How we shudder, weep and wail,
At the angel's noiseless beckoning,
　　At the lifting of the veil!

To the Infinite Creator
　　The grand Universe is one—
Far blue corridors are linking
　　Sea and sky and star and sun;
It is all the Father's mansion,
　　And the loved our hearts bewail,
Did but reach an inner chamber,
　　At the lifting of the veil!

Though we may not hear their footsteps,
　　As they journey to and fro,
Through the hidden, shining chambers,
　　Noiseless as the dropping snow—

Though we may not see their vestments
　Silvery pure as moonbeams pale,
We shall meet them fair as morning,
　At the lifting of the veil.

With His visible works so mighty—
　With such splendors spread abroad,
What must be the secret places
　Of this Palace of our God?
Not with anguish—not with weeping—
　But with raptures should we hail
Every beckoning of the angels,
　Every lifting of the veil!

THRENODY.

IN MEMORY OF THE LATE COL. E. D. BAKER.

BY MRS. E. A. SIMONTON PAGE.

UPON the battle-field,
'Mid charging squadrons rushing to and fro,
The soldier all undaunted by the foe,
　　To death must yield.
　　One moment on his ear,
　　Strike sharp and clear
The trumpet's clangor and wild throb of
　　drum;
And then the lips that woke the battle-cheer,
　　Through a swift prayer grow dumb.
　　One moment of sharp pain,
　　A sudden, gushing, crimson stain,
Then all unheeded falls the fiery rain,
　　And comrades moan anear!

"Brave heart and gallant leader," and tried
　　man,
True 'mid the truest, 'mong the greatest,
　　great!
Like one large heart the people mourn thy
　　fate,

With tears that drop like rain.
Hushed is the fervid eloquence that ran
Like syllabled lightning through the listener's
    brain;
    Mute are the lips and cold,
That held o'er language mastery intense,
  And coined the mind's rare opulence
      To dropping gold.
    Rare lips, grown mute and cold,
Henceforth your marble silence is not vain!
  No voice that with resistless might,
    Hath plead for God, and truth, and right,
      Can ever die—
Its echoes vibrate from eternity!

Statesman and patriot! thy great soul was
    stirred
With fealty that disdained the empty word,
    And lived in deeds;
Like mother slain by parricidal hands,
    Our hapless country bleeds.
But when her triumph sounds through all the
    lands,
    When deeper-rooted Liberty
Hath mined the tottering thrones of tyranny,
    Till awed, the despot stands,

Then shall thy name
Flash out through history like a flame,
          As one of those
Who, with prophetic voice and gleaming
          sword,
Hurled proud defiance at the Union's foes,
          And fell deplored.

Onward the solemn century rolls—
          Again the horologe of Time
Points to an hour appalling yet sublime,
          Which tries men's souls.
The "*dulce patria mori*" of the past,
          Rings like a bugle blast
From lips like thine, just dropping into
          dust—
Inspires to sacrifice and mightier deeds,
          And a devouter trust.
Through storm, "the Genius of America
          leads
Her sons to Freedom,"—and the pitiless
          storm
Beat on thy heart, impassioned, true and
          warm,
Stilling its pulses; but thou art not dead,
          Though priestly prayer be said.

The solemn-watching Past majestic stands,
Beckoning the Present with imploring hands,
    And up with lofty tread,
One after one, the nation's brave, like thee,
Climb the red path to Immortality.

    Rest, noble warrior, rest!
The darksome wounds in brow and breast,
    That stilled the loyal breath,
Far more than sumptuous praises of a king,
Shall keep thy memory sweetly blossoming,
And guard a hero's honor green in death.
Who dies for Freedom hath not died too
    soon,
Be it at morn, or eve, or life's high noon;
    And thou wert stricken down,
With silvered hair—true manhood's royal
    crown—
    So thou wert blest;
    At Heaven's supreme behest
Thy soul from conflict found a swift release,
    Thy latest victory won;
Pitched is thy tent beyond the setting sun,
    On the white shores of Peace.

POEMS.

BY MRS. E. A. SIMONTON PAGE.

ONLY through melodious utterance poets
  stand confessed and crowned,
Yet some souls make life-long music in a
  rhythmic hush profound.

The wide universe is a poem, marvelous as
  the Infinite mind ;
Star-worlds are the golden strophes, filled
  with splendors un-divined.

Soul-fraught poems in carved marbles speak
  rebuke for wrongs of men,
Where the tablet is enduring, and the chisel
  is the pen.

Harmonic poems, wordless, vibrant, a divine
  impulsion own,
Lifting up the listening peoples one step
  nearer to the Throne.

Iliads in prismatic colors, on the glowing can-
 vas tell
Truths profound to climes and ages by a
 speech made visible.

Every pure deed is a poem which recording
 angels name,
Tracing it on scrolls of sapphire in imperish-
 able flame.

Waning cycles may list vainly for a bardic
 voice supreme,
Yet true lives are grander epics than the
 mightiest poets dream.

UNDER THE PERSIMMON.

BY EMILIE LAWSON.

As the oak flames on the lawn,
I think of an autumn gone,
An Indian summer-time—the ripe October;
The forests were a-blaze,
The blue sky all a-haze,
And only the fair fields turned brown and
sober.

When cousin Madge and I—
Dear gipsy, sweet and sly,
Wandered across the fields—the fields of
stubble—
The sun through red mists shone,
Looking as if 'twere blown
From a magician's pipe—a rosy bubble.

We sat beneath a tree—
"Oh, Harry dear!" cried she,
"What is that fruit o'erhead so ripe and
yellow?

Pray climb and pluck me some!"
I answered "Tis a plum
Of a most luscious flavor, sweet and mellow."

Then up the tree I sped,
And showered about her head
This sour false fruit—false fruit that looked
        delicious;
She took one little bite—
Oh, the exquisite spite
That shook her dainty fist, so small—so
        vicious!

She shook that fist at me;
I cried, from up the tree,
"Sweetheart! sweetheart! I very well re-
        member
The purple plums I ate—
Purple and delicate,
From this same tree—and only last Decem-
        ber.

"Could it have been the snow?
Oh dearest, don't frown so!
Was it the frost or snow that made them
        sweeter,

As hearts in sharp distress
Lose half their bitterness,
Finding in woe a faith and hope completer?

I think I see her yet,
Her sweet mouth in a pet,
All puckered up with anger and persimmon;
I tried to moralize—
She scorned me with those eyes—
Those eyes that made her peerless among
    women.

Then down the tree I came,
Called coaxingly her name;
She stormed at first, then sobbed, and called
    me cruel,
And named one Reuben Guy
That loved her more than I—
At which I hinted mildly of a duel.

And then there came a mist,
In which I think we kissed—
It seems quite real, yet very, very dreamy;
A dream of red wine floods,
Of spicy scarlet buds,
And tropic blossoms soft and bland and
    creamy:

Time gliding as a boat
On pearly ponds afloat—
A heaven of heavens—her tender love its
        portal;
Oh beautiful strange dream—
How far its pictures seem—
For I am desolate, and she immortal.

All left to my despair
This flake of dusky hair,
And wild vine tendrils o'er a low grave
        groping;
Where, at her fast-shut door,
Shut from me evermore,
Was ended all my dreaming—all my hoping.

12

DREAM-TIME.

BY EMILIE LAWSON.

Alone I watch the dying day,
I see its tints of orange paling;
And just beyond the ruffled bay,
Gray mists the purple hills are veiling;
Upon the roof weird fingers play,
And all the winds are full of wailing.

Life's open book before me lies,
And, as I turn its leaves back faintly,
The pictures of the past arise;
Strange forms go by—appareled quaintly,
Sweet voices whisper, and dear eyes
Shine as of old—divine and saintly.

Once more I hear the gentle rhyme,
Where falling leaves still waters dimple,
The woods' low murmur, and the chime
Of silvery streamlets as they wimple—
And live again the golden time
Of childhood's joys—so pure and simple!

What pretty pebbles pave the creek,
The dear old creek by mulberries shaded!
There the shy frogs played hide-and-seek
Through lilies—with sweet spices laded;
And our wee shadows seemed to speak
From whispering wavelets, as we waded.

What leagues of nectar wooed the bees,
To buckwheat hills or dales of clover!
What twittering birds on blooming trees,
Cooed tenderly and played the lover!
While time with odorous breath of ease,
Told the delicious idyl over.

We reckoned then each year a gain;
Now they are counted with our losses;
Sharp thorns and thistles give us pain,
Where then we trod spring's velvet mosses;
Then, of our flowery garlands vain,
And now a-weary of our crosses.

I gathered wild flowers yesterday,
But somehow flowers have lost their sweet-
        ness;
Some quail were started—even they
Seemed to have lost their old discreetness,

And only hopped beside the way,
As if they had no need for fleetness.

But when I see the children meet,
Flower-laden, from their plays returning—
Care trampled by their heedless feet,
Their trustful souls all shadow spurning—
Their hearts wild with impatient beat,
And hope's bright fires within them burn-
    ing—

I know life blooms the same, but I
Shall breath its old-time fragrance—never!
The dreary Now—the dear Gone-by,
The bridgeless floods of sorrow sever.
Ah, me! how wistfully I sigh
For dream-time lost—and lost forever.

STAR-TIME.

BY EMILIE LAWSON.

DEAR heart! I watch yon slowly-setting star
   With such a weary feeling of unrest!
And thou art watching, too, so far, so far
   Beyond the purple mountain of the west!
I mark its trembling rays of pale red light
   Bridge the dim amber of the sunset steep;
Now comes the sweet hour of our old good-
      night,
   Then kiss me, dear, before I go to sleep.

For what to me are evening's marvelous
      dyes,
   With all the glimmerings of the sunset
      slopes,
If from their light I turn to meet thine eyes,
   And find thee not, thou one hope of my
      hopes!
As thoughts fly over leagues of land and sea,
   Or lightnings compass mountains with a
      leap,
So when the night falls, come thou unto me,
   To kiss me, love, before I go to sleep.

And life's best joys are never more than this,
   A faithful friend, whose true heart makes
      us blest;
The exquisite fervor of a holy kiss,
   Whose breath is fragrance, and whose
      touch is rest!
Dearer the pure, pale odorous way-side rose
   Than all the golden grain we sow and
      reap;
Dearer than daylight's gain the daylight's
   close,
With love's fond kiss before we go to sleep.

And when the summer's leaves are sere and
      brown,
   And wintry winds weep through her faded
      dells,
When all the scarlet rays of life go down,
   And angel's tongue death's wondrous poem
      tells,
Give me this token e'er we two shall part,
   Forever and ever in the heavens to keep;
Come to me then, thou fond dream of my
      heart,
   With one last kiss before I go to sleep.

ASPIRATION.

BY CARRIE CARLTON.

HERE let me rest, upon the dewy sod,
　Beneath the generous shade of forest trees,
And cool awhile life's fever in my heart,
　Laving my spirit in this morning breeze.
Take me to your embrace, ye shadowy glades!
　And sunny mound rise up 'twixt me and
　　　life;
Sweet mother—Nature—fold your child once
　　more
　To your warm heart, I'm weary of the
　　strife.

I'm weary of the dusty march of days,
　The clamor of the city's eager throng,
The strife of man against his brother man,
　The pigmy Right against the giant Wrong.
To this sweet spot my yearning spirit turns,
　And my freed soul unfolds her wings for
　　flight;
Thy brightest bauble has no charm, O world,
　Can tempt my heart, and rival this delight.

In the grand stillness of this solemn shade,
  I lay my earth-stained brow upon the sod,
And by the precious right that He has given,
  Send the soul's incense up to nature's God.
All ties of earth are loosened, naught appears
    To claim one thought from me beneath
        the sky;
Yet stay—one heart-string is unbroken yet,
  And vibrates to divinest melody.

Oh, yes! there is among the throng of men,
    One voice that I would bend from Heav-
        en to hear,
One eye, whose glance would draw my spirit
        back,
    If it had entered the celestial sphere;
One heart whose faintest throb would reach
        my ear,
    Though folded deep within the grove's
        embrace.
Come back, my winged soul, earth claims me
        still,
    God help me! lest I wish no other place.

THE FALL OF CHARLESTON.

BY CARRIE CARLTON.

MOTHER, dear, the guns are firing, all day
    long, with ceaseless roar,
And the men, with eager faces, tell some story
    o'er and o'er;   .
All the pretty flags are waving up and down
    the street to-day—
What can make them all so happy?   Darling
    mother, tell me, pray.

That, my son, is news of victory, that the
    laughing bells repeat;
And 'tis joy that makes the people with loud
    cheers each other greet,
For the news that thrilled our country as the
    cannons shook the air,
With a hope that was thanksgiving, and a
    faith that was a prayer—
Telling that our flag is waving over Charles-
    ton's rebel towers,
And her conquered hosts were fleeing fast
    before the march of ours;

12*

That her haughty head is lying in the dust
    beneath our stars,
And a crimson victory covers our brave he-
    roes' wounds and scars;
That the red, right hand of treason, in defi-
    ance first laid bare
O'er the altar-fires of Charleston, now lies
    prone and withered there.
Prone the shackled limbs of treason lie resist-
    less in the dust,
By the very shrines whose fires nursed it into
    being first;
And our armies—God uphold them—march
    with steady step along,
Trusting, through their mighty leader, with
    the right to quell the wrong.
That's the story of the joy-bells, and the
    banners gleaming bright—
Why so thoughtful, Louie darling, was it not
    a bonnie sight?

Mother dear, it must be bonnie, for your
    face grows bright with joy,
As you tell the thrilling story to your loving
    little boy.

I can see the red glow coming through the
    pale drift of your cheek,
And your eyes grow bright and sparkle as the
    welcome words you speak;
Your sweet voice is always sweeter when the
    night begins to fall—
I could listen on forever—darling mother, is
    that *all?*

Hush, my darling! nestle closer in my shel-
    tering arms to-night;
Why should you be told of sorrow, and de-
    struction's withering blight?
That's the bright side of the story; my sweet
    boy will later know
All the dreadful tale of anguish that has rent
    our country so;
You will learn it soon and sadly, and I dare
    not cloud your brow,
With one shade of coming sorrow, 'tis so
    bright and sunny now.
But my heart is aching, aching, underneath
    the joy you see,
And an under-tone of heart-break in the joy-
    bells rang to me;

For my heart was ever thinking of the *fallen*
    in the strife,
None of ours, thank God, but cherished by
    some mother, sister, wife.
O, my boy, there's not a soldier falls amid
    our myriad slain,
And lies wounded, gasping, dying, on the
    reeking battle-plain,
But has left *some* hearts to mourn him—hearts
    that bleed but may not speak,
Save the weary, soul-sick language of the
    sunken, pallid cheek—
Hearth-stones desolate forever, white hairs
    drifting to the grave;
This is why some hearts are breaking, though
    the banners proudly wave.

Men must only look to glory; their's the
    part to do and dare;
And we must not think to have them all our
    tender yearnings share.
But 'tis meet that *we* should sorrow at the
    story, fierce and wild,
We are so unused to terror—I a woman, you
    a child;

So we'll softly weep together for the poor
heart-broken ones
Who hear the knell of life's bright dream in
victory's echoing guns.
And my darling boy, remember—'tis your
mother's voice you hear—
By the holy tie that binds us, in your heart
these words revere.
When the after-days of plenty, and of smiling peace shall dawn,
When our country's stars shall glimmer,
every cloud of treason gone,
When rebellion's dead forever—then remember in your joy,
The price your country paid for peace—*the
price of victory, boy.*

PURIFIED.

BY CARRIE CARLTON.

"Once I was pure as the snow—but I fell!
Fell like the snow-flakes from heaven to hell;
Fell, to be trampled like filth in the street;
Fell, to be scoffed, to be spit on and beat."
  —*From the Poem of The "Beautiful Snow."*

CROUCHED in an archway, cold and bare,
Famished and chilled with the wintry air,
And mantled alone with her long dark hair,
  A woman lay;
A woman that once was pure and white,
As the angels that stand in the presence bright
Of the Undefiled; but souls of light
  Are cased in clay.

She lay on the cold, unpitying stones,
But past was the hour of sighs and groans;
Her heart was breaking with tears and moans,
  As the snow came down.
"Once I was pure as the snow!" she said;
"Oh, pitying God, that I were dead!
With the snow I am lying beneath the tread
  Of the heartless town."

The white snow, trodden by passing feet,
Grew foul and black, and o'er the street
Soon flowed in many a darksome sheet—
   Impure and cold.
Then came the frosty midnight air—
A miracle, lo! on the gutter there,
'Twas changed to a chrysolite, pure and fair—
   Spotless of mould.

The woman's eyes, with their fading gleam,
Saw a wondrous hope in the changing stream;
And low she murmured, as in a dream—
   "Sweet Saviour, hear!"
Then over her visage wan there stole
A still, calm beauty, as though her soul
No longer was subject to sin's control,
   Nor doubt, nor fear.

The morning sun threw a crimson glow
O'er the holy scene that was spread below,
Where, wrapped in a mantle of spotless snow,
   A woman died;
Where a soul uprose from the frozen clay,
And upward, heavenward, winged its way,
All tarnish of evil washed away—
   Redeemed and purified.

"IS IT COME?" IT IS COME.

BY MRS. S. M. CLARKE.

Ay, *it* is come!—the world's long prom-
    ised day!
It dawned, O, Syria, on thy night of years,
When tyrants ruled thee with despotic sway,
    And earth was deluged with thy mothers'
        tears.
The "wise men" saw the gleaming of its
    star—
The star of love, the herald of its morn,
And westward turned to follow it afar,
    And watch the breaking light that did the
        age adorn.

The "Sun of Righteousness" arose on earth
    To warm the *crouching millions* into life,
Oppressed by kings and priests—e'en from
        their birth
    Condemned to life-long toil and ceaseless
        strife;
Then was the Chrism, the anointing oil,
    On our humanity poured from above,

And *we* were crowned, daughters and sons
    of toil,
All Kings and Priests of God—heirs of
    the Father's love.

But clouds of error dimmed its early light,
    And Superstition cast a deeper shade;
Emerging from the dread, chaotic night
    That ignorance and human woe had made.
Yet higher it arose and brighter beamed,
    Revealing life immortal to the world!
Far o'er Internum's waves sublimely streamed,
    And in Italia's sky the bannered cross un-
    furled.

Her warrior Kings paid homage to the cross,
  · But, in the name of *Heaven,* their armies
    led
To spoil, and bloody strife, and reckless
    loss
    Of *Heaven's* despairing millions meanly
    fed!
While hireling Priests, with bold and im-
    pious thought,
    Attempted to monopolize the light,

That beamed for *all*, their heritage unbought,
　And in sepulchral cells withdraw it from
　　the sight.

Cells where the lamp of Knowledge feebly
　shone
　For the usurping few—and there to dole,
For gold and penance, wrung with many a
　groan,
　　Just light enough to save "the ruined soul!"
They proudly boasted then, 'fore earth and
　heaven,
　All light · and truth were captives of the
　　hours,
And to *their* regal head, alone, was given,
　As God's anointed One, illimitable power.

The "Sun of Righteousness" ascended still.
　Buried 'neath fretted vaults, to creeds a
　　prey,
They saw no splendor rest on Zion's hill,
　And called cathedral gloom "the prom-
　　ised day."
Westward its steady course the Christ-light
　kept,
　And on Britannia's Isles in glory broke!

Immortal Genius, that for ages slept,
　　Unfolded her bright wings, once more on
　　　earth awoke.

And, where her shadow glanced upon the
　　sod,
　　Embryo Art and Science sprang to birth;
And great Philosophy, serene like God,
　　Familiar converse held with sons of earth.
The cowering millions heard, with deep
　　heart-throes,
　　The truth that made them free—sublimely,
　　　then,
Inspired with hope, forgetful of their woes,
　　They shook their trammels off, and walked
　　　erect like men.

Thy monuments of deathless fame arose,
　　Prouder than Egypt's in her Pharaohs'
　　　days,
Or Grecia's temples in sublime repose,
　　Above the murmuring crowds that throng-
　　　ed her ways,
O, Europe, then!—vast monuments of
　　thought,
　　Immortal aspirations rose to heaven,

Whose spirit columns richly were inwrought
  With priceless gems of mind thy God had
    freely given.

But when thy Kings and Priests, in evil
    hour,
  Their fetters forged for freeborn mind
    again,
They roused a spirit mightier than their
    power,
  To check their pride, their tyranny re-
    strain.
The "Pilgrims" launched their bark upon
    the sea,
  Forsaking "Father-land," dear kindred
    ties,
And *westward* turned, America, to thee,
  "Inalienable rights" to seek 'neath freer
    skies!   .

From its deep centre shook the moral world,
  Rending the tie 'tween rulers and the ruled,
When the brave "Pilgrim band" their flag
    unfurled,
  In "higher law" of *human rights* well
    schooled!

Grim DESPOTISM hoary, bowed his head
  Upon his ancient throne, the people's
    scorn—
INTOLERANCE shrieked out with pain and
    dread,
  And in the mighty throe Democracy was
    born!

WESTWARD the Christ-light kept its glorious
    way!
WESTWARD fair Liberty her altars reared!
WESTWARD Equality bore gentle sway!—
  The *many* there the *few* no longer feared.
Accepted was "the brotherhood of man,"
  The School-house and the Church rose
    side by side,
Open to all, upon the heavenly plan,
  With knowledge to enlighten, truth divine
    to guide.

Ay, *it* is come!—"the world's long promised
    day!"
  Its signs behold, O, faint and doubting
    heart!—

The People frame the laws they will obey,
  And wield the wealth of the great public
    mart.
And from the People spring the chosen few
  To execute the People's sovereign will—
"Old things have passed away, and all are
    new"—
  The humble and the poor the seats of honor fill.

Millions in ignorant poverty and shame
  No longer toil from youth to helpless
    years,
.To crown a Despot with immortal fame,
  Whose reign was a sad reign of human
    tears;
But millions, for the millions, work and
    thrive—
  For them the Farmer reaps the golden
    grain—
For them the Sculptor bids the marble live—
  And bold Discoverer tracks the distant,
    pathless main.

For them the Inventor tasks his giant pow-
    ers—
  For them the Student burns the midnight
    oil

For them the Artist spends his youthful
hours,
And weaves bright garlands for the sons
of toil.
For them the Poet plumes his eagle wings,
To catch the anthem of angelic spheres,
And soaring heavenward, "ever soaring,
sings"—
"*Labor is worship*" meet, thro' the eternal
years.

Ay, *it is come!*—"the world's long promised
day;"
And WESTWARD still the path of Empire
leads,
To California's rock-bound shores away—
Far, far away o'er mountains and o'er
meads,
Where the "Lone Star" of the Pacific shines,
To lure the traveler to that land of gold,
Where earth locks up within her secret mines,
For future generations, her vast wealth
untold.

Where flowers of every hue and every clime,
In regal beauty their tiaras rear,

And primal trees aspire to heights sublime,
  In green old age of many a hundred year
Where lavish nature to the laborer yields,
  Of vegetation, marvelous in growth,
Supplies exhaustless from her fruitful fields,
  Where summer's lingering sun rivals the
    genial south.

O, California! young each passing year,
  And yet a giant in thy youthful might,
Pause for a moment in thy swift career,
  And dedicate thy strength to. *God and
    Right!*
I see, e'en now, thy guardian Genius stand
  Sublimely forth in all her maiden pride,
The Empress of the sea and of the land—
  While thro' the conquered air her winged
    coursers ride.

Benign and calm as Deity, her mein—
  Toward the south she turns an earnest
    eye—
Her robe is brightly flecked with ocean sheen,
  And on her brow the glory of the sky.
One hand, upraised, a magic trident grasps,
  Insignia of her power and triple sway—

The book of fate the other firmly clasps—
  Her will omnipotent, earth, sea, and air
    obey.

The sister Arts are grouped in beauty near,
  With thoughtful Science who their work
    commands.
Labor, with sinewy arm, the pioneer
  Of mighty nations, in the fore-ground
    stands,
With great Invention, busy with his plan
  To lighten toil, control resisting earth
And elements, to will of lordly man—
  As Providence decreed at the Creation's
    birth.

Thy Genius points her sceptre toward the
    waste
  Of hill and vale, and far-extending plain—
And the down-trodden of the nations ha▉,
  And gardens bloom, and fields of waving
    grain,
She turns it westward toward the open sea,
  And all its thousand isles are winged with
    fleet

13

That skim the crested billows, wild and free,
  To lay their richest treasures proudly at
    her feet.

Fill up the vallies! bring the mountains
    low!
  Ye hardy toilers for the golden ore,
Make straight the highway of the nations, lo!
  The eagles flock from every distant shore!
The anointed sons of Genius swiftly come
  To the MERIDIAN of "the promised
    day"—
Our God hath given another Eden home—
  Sons of the "Pilgrim band," prepare the
    nations' way.

PALMA.

BY FRANCES FULLER VICTOR.

WHAT tellest thou to heaven
   Thou royal tropic tree?
At morn, or noon, or even,
   Proud dweller by the sea,
What is thy song to heaven?

The homesick heart that fainted
   In torrid sun and air,
With peace becomes acquainted
   Beholding thee so fair—
With joy becomes acquainted;

And charms itself with fancies
   About thy kingly race—
With gay and wild romances
   That mimic thee in grace
Of supple, glorious fancies.

I feel thou art not tender,
   Scion of sun and sea;

The wild bird does not render
  To thee its minstrelsy,
Feeling thou art not tender,

But calm, serene, and saintly,
  As high-born things should be;
Who if they love us faintly,
  Make us love reverently,
Because they are so saintly.

To be loved without loving,
  O proud and princely palm!
Is to fancy our ship moving
  With the ocean at dead calm—
The joy of love is loving.

Because the sun did sire thee,
  The ocean nurse thy youth;
Because the stars desire thee,
  The warm winds whisper truth,
Shall nothing ever fire thee?

What is thy tale to heaven
  In the sultry, tropic noon?
What whisperest thou at even
  To the dusky Indian moon?
Has she sins to be forgiven?

Keep all her secrets—loyal,
    As only great souls are—
As only souls most royal,
    To the flower or to the star
Alike are purely loyal.

O Palma, if thou hearest,
    Thou proud and princely tree!
Thou knowest that my dearest
    Is emblemed forth in thee—
My kingly palm, my dearest.

I am his moon, admiring,
    His waving wind, his star;
And I glory in desiring
    My palm-tree from afar—
    Glad as happier lovers are—
Am happy in desiring.

EL PALO SANTO.

BY FRANCES FULLER VICTOR.

In the deep woods of Mexico,
  Where screams the painted paraquet,
Where mocking birds flit to and fro,
  With borrowed notes they half forget;
Where brilliant flowers and poisonous vines
  Are mingled in a firm embrace,
And the same gaudy plant entwines
  Some reptile of a venomed race;
Where spreads the Itos' chilly shade,
  Benumbing even in summer's heat,
The weary traveler who hath laid
  Himself to noonday slumbers sweet;
Where skulks unseen the beast of prey—
  The native robber glares and hides—
And treacherous death keeps watch alway
  For him who flies or him who bides.

In the deep tropic woods there grows,
  A tree whose tall and silvery bole,
Above the dusky forest shows
  As shining as a saintly soul,

Among the souls of sinful men,
   Lifting its milk-white flowers to heaven,
And breathing incense out, as when
   Earth's almost sinless ones are shriven.

The skulking robber drops his eyes,
   And signs himself with holy cross,
If far, between him and the skies,
   He sees its pearly blossoms toss:
The wanderer halts to gaze upon
   The lovely vision far and near,
And smiles and sighs to think of one,
   He wishes for the moment here.

Nor Mexic native fears the fang,
   The poisoned vine, the venomed bee,
If he may soothe the baleful pang
   With juices from his "holy tree."

How do we all in life's wild ways,
   Which oft we traverse lost and lone,
Need that which heavenward draws the gaze,
   Some Palo Santo of our own!

SUNSET AT THE MOUTH OF THE COLUMBIA.

BY FRANCES FULLER VICTOR.

THERE sinks the sun; like cavalier of old,
    Servant of crafty Spain,
He flaunts his banner, barred with blood and
       gold,
    Wide o'er the western main.
A thousand spear-heads glint beyond the
      trees,
    In columns bright and long;
While kindling fancy hears upon the breeze
    The swell of shout and song!

And yet not here Spain's gay, adventurous
      host
    Dipped sword, or planted cross;
The treasures guarded by this rock-bound
      coast,
    Counted them gain nor loss.

The blue Columbia, sired by the eternal hills
    And wedded with the sea,
O'er golden sands, tithes from a thousand
    rills,
    Rolled in lone majesty—

Through deep ravine, through burning, bar-
    ren plain,
    Through wild and rocky strait,
Through forest dark, and mountains rent in
    twain,
    Toward the sunset gate,
While curious eyes, keen with the lust of
    gold,
    Caught not the informing gleam;
These mighty breakers age on age have rolled
    To meet this mighty stream.

Age after age these noble hills have kept
    The same majestic lines;
Age after age the horizon's edge been swept
    By fringe of pointed pines.
Summers and winters circling came and went,
    Bringing no change of scene;
Unresting and unhasting, and unspent,
    Dwelt Nature here serene,

13*

Till God's own time to plant of Freedom's
     seed
  In his selected soil,
Denied forever unto blood and greed,
  But blest to honest toil.
There sinks the sun.   Gay cavalier! no more
  His banners trail the sea,
And all his legions shining on the shore
  Fade into mystery.

The swelling tide laps on the shingly beach
  Like any starving thing;
And   hungry   breakers, white with wrath,
     upreach
  In a vain clamoring.
The shadows fall; just level with mine eye
  Sweet Hesper stands and shines,
And shines beneath an arc of golden sky,
  Pinked round with pointed pines.

A noble scene! all breadth, deep tone and
     power,
  Suggesting glorious themes,
Shaming the idler who would fill the hour
  With unsubstantial dreams.

Be mine the dreams prophetic, shadowing
    forth
  The things that yet shall be,
When through this gate the treasures of the
    North
  Flow outward to the sea.

LUELLA.

BY ELIZA A. PITTSINGER.

"Oh, touch the harp gently, Luella has
    gone!
In her beauty and grace, like a star from the
    dawn—
Oh speak of her softly, for deep in my breast
Lies buried a sorrow that robs me of rest—
Unheeding, serenely and blindly she stole
The light from the morning—the life from
    my soul.
        Luella, my dearest,
           My brightest and best,
        Oh, why didst thou waken
           My soul and my rest?
        Luella, the queenly,
           The peerless and free,
        Oh why hast thou taken
           Thy presence from me?
        Say, why didst thou waken
           The life of my soul—
        The love that around me
           So peacefully stole?

Thy beauty that bound me,
Oh, where has it flown—
The love that so bound me
In soul to thine own?"

"Oh, grieve not, thou loved one! in patience
    I wait
Thy coming beyond the dim regions of
    Fate;
The love that lies bleeding, the bliss that
    has flown,
Through sorrow shall make thee more dearly
    mine own—
        Arise, then, and grieve not,
            Oh grieve not thy fate'
        Beyond the dim portal
            Thy coming I wait—
        The star of the morning
            Thy presence hath flown,
        Ere the light of its dawning
            Hath made me thine own;
        But the love that united
            My soul unto thine,
        So cruelly blighted,
            Immortal doth shine—

The presence that fondly
Thy soul did entwine,
The love that so won thee,
And made thee divine,
The rapture that blended
In love and delight,
Hath newly ascended
And I bathe in its light—
I drink of the fountain,
And lave in the streams
That leap from the mountain,
And my soul it redeems
From that moment of madness,
The pain of that night,
When in sorrow and sadness
I fled from thy sight;
Arise, then, and grieve not, oh grieve never-
more!
For Luella is waiting beyond the dim shore,
Where the sorrow of parting, the tones of
despair,
Awake not the thrill of the balm-scented air;
Where the breath of the morning in rapture
exhales
To music that lingers in love-breathing vales,

And the warble of birds, and the play of the
   stream,   .
Are sweeter by far than the Orient's dream—
'Tis the bright summer-land—'tis the land
   of the morn!
Where the soul to new beauty and glory is
   born—
There is life in its waters, and joy in its
   breeze,
Delight in its verdure, and balm in its trees,
A glow in its morn, and a blush in its eve,
More pensive and soft than the fancy can
   weave—
'Tis the home of the spirit—the bright
   morning land,
In its heaven of beauty, transcendent and
   grand,
Where the soul from its orbit of pleasure
   and pain,
In its wisdom and glory triumphant shall
   reign;
Arise, then, and grieve not, oh grieve never-
   more!
I await for thy coming beyond the dim
   shore;

Arise from thy sorrow,
   Awake from the night,
The light of the morrow
   Shall gleam on thy sight!
Arise from thy sadness,
   Awake from thy woe,
The light of my spirit
   Around, thee doth glow!
The rays that entwine thee
   Immortally shine,
In my soul I enshrine thee,
   And make thee divine!"

"Oh touch the harp gently, Luella, my
   love—
Speaks hope to my soul from the pure
   realms above—
She lives, oh she lives, this angel of mine,
My own destined bride, immortal, divine."

TWILIGHT FANCIES.

BY ELIZA A. PITTSINGER.

Softly flit the fairy fancies
  Through the sunlight of my brain,
Weaving webs of weird romances
  In a laughing, joyous strain—
      Gently creeping,
      Gaily leaping,
Twilight revels strangely keeping
      In my brain.

Ere the evening lamps are lighted,
  While my soul is wrapt in thought,
Wait they not to be invited,
  Quite unwelcome and unsought—
      Never sitting,
      Ever flitting,
All the earnestness outwitting
      Of my thought.

Thus to have my being haunted
  By these fairies, all astray,
By these elfin-sprites enchanted,
  Is a spell upon my way,

That shall borrow
For the morrow,
All the pleasure and the sorrow
Of to-day.

In my hours of quiet musing,
By these phantoms thus caressed
I have lost the right of choosing
As I ought, my favored guest—
Uninvited,
Often slighted,
Come they when the lamps are lighted
For a guest.

Thus they come, the fairy fancies,
Laughing, flitting through my brain,
Weaving webs of weird romances,
In a wayward, joyous strain—
Gaily creeping,
Madly leaping,
Even now their revels keeping
In my brain.

MARCH IN CALIFORNIA.

BY MRS. M. D. STRONG.

It brings no blast of the storm-king,
  No sound of the driving snow,
It groups us not at the fire-side
  To bask in the ruddy glow.

But soft and warm pours the sunshine
  All day from a heaven so blue,
And young leaves toy with the light wind
  That steals from their cheeks the dew.

The red-breast sings on the oak bough,
  The wild duck is out on the bay,
The lark springs up from the hill-side
  And with swift wing darts away.

'Mid springing grass on the upland,
  Where the star-flower buds peep up,
With folded wing sits the blue bird
  And drinks from the butter-cup.

In the emerald robe of the valley,
  The golden violet shines,
And the orchis, wreathed with the blue bell,
  In gorgeous broidery twines.

O month, that cold to the East-land
  The breath of the storm dost bring,
To us thy days are the fete days
  In the glorious reign of spring.

NIGHT ON CALIFORNIA'S HILLS.

BY ANNE H. FADER

'Tis night on California's hills,
    And o'er her valleys green,
A holy calmness now distills
    Its essence o'er the scene;
And up the winding steps of stars,
    And through the milky spray,
Past many a track of golden cars,
    The moon walks on her way.

The dark pine throws its impress tall,
    In fretted shade and sheen,
Against the yielding azure wall
    That canopies the scene;
And autumn's spirit moves around,
    With shadows on its wing;
It seemeth but a schoolboy's bound
    Since late we hailed the spring.

But now October's robes of brown
    Are sometimes fluttering chill,
As swifter now the sun goes down
    Behind the shadowy hill.

And now the half-chilled autumn clouds
  Float dark before the wind,
Presages of the wintry shrouds
  That soon will cramp and bind.

But California's towering hills
  Shall never shrink with cold,
And California's creeks and rills
  No fetters long shall hold:
And, from these grand old hills and trees,
  There yet may come a sound,
That shall re-echo o'er the seas,
  Where'er man treads the ground.

Her destiny must still be on,
  While rolling skies are blue,
And glory on the heads shall dawn
  Of children nobly true—
If all along the mighty track
  Of ages yet to be,
No heart shall fail, no hand shall slack,
  To keep her spirit free!

And calmly still yon faithful moon,
  With eye unmoved and vast,
Shall see earth's proudest glories loom
  And sink away at last;

While human eyes that sparkle now,
　And hearts that fondly dream,
Before the hand of years must bow,
　And leave the varied scene.

Yet more immortal than the ray
　That gilds yon mountain's brow,
More glorious than the cloud-piled way,
　Night's orbs are circling now.
Shall these white spirits, washed in blood,
　And robed in taintless snow,
Ascend to him who poured the flood,
　And hung the promise-bow?

This be our aim, this be our end,
　The only high and pure,
That when earth's grandest fabrics rend,
　Shall stand more firmly sure:
And faithful let our footsteps move,
　To that unfading shore,
Where Zion's heights to us shall prove
　A home forevermore!

THE LAST EARNEST WISH.

BY ANNIE A. FITZGERALD.

I KNOW by the fainter pulse of my heart,
  And the cold of my wasted brow,
By the chill that is not of the summer wind,
  That my life-strength is ebbing low.
By the shadows that flit in their shapeless
    forms,
  ` Twixt me and the June-day skies—
By the shadows that here in this noontide
    hour,
  Are hiding the light from my eyes.

Come nearer, my husband, and let me place
  My hands in thy gentle clasp;
They are bloodless and thin, and they soon
    shall be cold,
  In the power of a mightier grasp.
Bend nearer, my husband, my tones must be
    low,
  For the strength of my voice is no more,
And I yet have a boon I must crave from
    thy love,
  Ere the last of my struggles are o'er.

I know that it matters not where I shall rest,
  When these faint-throbbing pulses are
    still;
But I shudder to think that my body must
    sleep,
  Where all is so dreary and chill.
'Tis my last wish to thee—'tis the last of my
    life,
  Brought back by this cool summer breeze,
Will you lay me to rest where the sunlight
    will fall,
  Through the leaves of the shadowy trees?

Where the fresh flowers may bloom and the
    wild birds may sing,
  As half in regret o'er my lot,
Where the dead leaves of autumn shall sigh
    o'er my grave,
  When my name and my love are forgot.
When thy heart is estranged—nay, pledge
    me no faith,
  That thy future may sadly regret,—
When another shall claim all thy cares and
    thy smiles,
  Thou hadst loved—but thou too canst
    forget!

14

Oh! I would be remembered—then lay me
    to rest,
  Where the sunlight its tracing weaves,
Where the night-winds, less fickle than hu-
    man resolves,
  Will sigh out a dirge mid the leaves.
Where the moonlight shall steal with a kind-
    lier gleam,
  And the tears of the winter shall flow,
When the eyes that may weep o'er my loss
    for awhile,
  Shall be lit with a happier glow.

Is this cold on my brow—is this chill in my
    heart,
  From the breath of the soft summer
    breeze?
Oh, will you remember our hopes and our
    dreams,
  When I sleep neath the shadowy trees?
Will you sometimes remember how dearly
    I loved,
  When you smile at another's light glee,
Will you sometimes remember my trembling
    lips breathed,
  "A life's dying blessing on thee?"

*   *   *   *   *   *   *

They laid her to rest where the chill damps
    of age,
  To the dark vault clings cheerless and
    drear,
And the smiles of another has brightened the
    home
  And the heart that she cherished so dear.

WAITING FOR THE RAIN.

BY ANNIE A. FITZGERALD.

Oh! the Earth is weary waiting,
    Waiting for the rain—
Waiting for the fresh'ning showers,
Wak'ning all her slumb'ring powers,
    With their dewy moisture sating
      Thirsty hill and plain.
Oh! the Earth is weary waiting,
    Waiting for the rain.

Oh! the Earth is weary longing,
    Longing for the rain—
Longing for the cloud-wrapt mountains,
Longing for the leaping fountains,
    With their clamorous murmurs thronging
      To the silent plain.
Oh! the Earth is weary longing,
    Longing for the rain.

Oh! the Earth is pained with throbbing,
    Throbbing for the rain—

Pained to see the valley fading—
Pained to see the frost's red braiding,
  And the with'ring north winds sobbing
    O'er her fields of grain.
Oh! the Earth is pained with throbbing,
    Throbbing for the rain.

    Oh! the Earth is sore with sighing,
      Sighing for the rain—
Sighing for the green grass springing,
And the fragrant wild flowers bringing
  Beauty—ere the clover dying
    Sear the waiting plain.
Oh! the Earth is sore with sighing,
    Sighing for the rain.

    Sore with restlessness and throbbing,
      Throbbing for the rain—
While along the upturned furrow
Busy rooks and blackbirds burrow,
  From her wide-spread gardens robbing
    Wealth of scattered grain.
Oh! the Earth is very weary,
    Waiting for the rain.

Waiting restlessly yet weary—
   Waiting for the rain,
For tne crystal tear-drops clinging,
To the wild oats, fresh upspringing,
   And the voices blending cheery
    With the wild-bird's strain.
Oh! the Earth is sad and weary,
   Waiting for the rain.

And our human hearts grow weary,
   Throbbing day by day—
Thirsting for the fresh'ning showers
O'er the dreams of future hours,
   While the present, never sating,
    Glides unfelt away.
Oh! the heart is weary, weary,
   Through its lifelong day.

THE SONG OF THE FLUME.

BY ANNA M. FITCH.

Awake, awake! for my track is red,
　With the glow of the coming day;
And with tinkling tread, from my dusky bed,
　I haste o'er the hills away,
Up from the valley, up from the plain,
　Up from the river's side;
For I come with a gush, and a torrent's rush,
　And there's wealth in my swelling tide.

I am fed by the melting rills that start
　Where the sparkling snow-peaks gleam,
My voice is free, and with fiercest glee
　I leap in the sun's broad beam;
Tho' torn from the channels deep and old,
　I have worn through the craggy hill,
Yet I flow in pride, as my waters glide,
　And there's mirth in my music still.

I sought the shore of the sounding sea,
　From the far Sierra's hight,
With a starry breast, and a snow-capped crest
　I foamed in a path of light;

But they bore me thence in a winding way,
　　They've fettered me like a slave,
And as scarfs of old were exchanged for
　　　　gold,
　　So they barter my soil-stained wave.

Thro' the deep tunnel, down the dark shaft,
　　I search for the shining ore ;
Hoist it away to the light of day,
　　Which it never has seen before.
Spade and shovel, mattock and pick,
　　Ply them with eager haste ;
For my golden shower is sold by the hour,
　　And the drops are too dear to waste.

Lift me aloft to the mountain's brow,
　　Fathom the deep "blue vein,"
And I'll sift the soil for the shining spoil,
　　As I sink to the valley again.
The swell of my swarthy breast shall bear
　　Pebble and rock away,
Though they brave my strength, they shall
　　　　yield at length,
　　But the glittering gold shall stay.

Mine is no stern and warrior march,
　No stormy trump and drum;
No banners gleam in my darkened stream,
　As with conquering step I come;
But I touch the tributary earth
　Till it owns a monarch's sway,
And with eager hand, from a conquered land,
　I bear its wealth away.

Awake, awake! there are loving hearts
　In the lands you've left afar;
There are tearful eyes in the homes you
　　prize
　As they gaze on the western star;
Then up from the valley, up from the hill,
　Up from the river's side;
For I come with a gush, and a torrent's rush,
　And there's wealth in my swelling tide.

14*

THE FLAG ON FIRE.*

BY ANNA M. FITCH.

Up the sombre
Silent chamber
Of the silver-seamed Sierra,
Where the Pi-ute
Roams in quiet,
And the eagle spreads her eyrie—
Climbed our flag, and sat in splendor
Thronged with elemental wonder.

Flushed with warning,
Dawned the morning,
O'er Nevada's gold-girt canons
While momentous
Clouds portentous
Beat aloft their dusky pinions,
And the lengthening day slow wheeling
'Neath its swarthy weight was reeling.

---

* From the summit of Mount Davidson, looking westward from Virginia City, Nevada, float the stars and stripes. On the evening of July 30th, 1863, upon the breaking away of a storm, this banner was suddenly illuminated by some curious refraction of the rays of the setting sun. Thousands of awe struck persons witnessed the spectacle, which continued until the streets of Virginia, 1500 feet below, were in utter darkness.

Now the marring
Lightning scarring,
Cleaves the mailed front of heaven,
Sifting, shifting,
Drifting, rifting,
Clouds capricious course till even,
So the swarthy army marches,
Conquering through the shadowy arches.

Cloud-bemantled,
Storm-ensandled,
Droops the flag, all gloom-encompassed,
Now unfurling,
Waltzing, whirling,
To the music of the tempest—
While aloft the dark-browed legion
Marshals through the storm-wrapped re-
gion.

Now the crumbling
Shadows, tumbling
Into silver-skirted showers,
Lo! upbuilded
From the gilded
Eastern crags, a rainbow towers;
Linked with Carson's purple fountain,
Circling desert, vale and mountain.

Fire! Fire!
Fire! Fire!
Who has set the flag on fire?
What vile traitor
By Creator
Spurned, thus dare defy despair?
God of prophecy and power,
Stay the omen of the hour.

Oh! the splendor,
Oh! the wonder,
To the worshiping beholder!
Gathering, glowing,
Flaming, flowing
Skyward—fiercer, freer, bolder
Burn the beating stars of empire,
Lit by traitor-torch, nor camp-fire.

Blood nor pallette,
More than all that,
Mid those starry embers linger;
Tis an omen,
Sent by no man—
Signet on an unseen finger—
Prophecy from heaven's own portal,
Borne by winged worlds immortal.

Now the circling
Darkness purpling,
Plumes the rock-ribbed mountain hoary;
Yet the hallowed
Flag unpillowed,
Burns aloft in stilly glory;
Wonder-mute, no man inveigheth;
Peace, be still! a nation prayeth.

A CHRISTMAS RHYME.

BY SARAH E. CARMICHAEL.

I GIVE you a rhyme for the Christmas time—
      Heigho!
Come pledge one cup, where the wine wells up,
     For a Christmas long ago:
When the merry shout of the winds rang out,
     While they danced with the falling snow,
And the clouds were rent from the firma-
    ment
    To mantle the world below.

I was rather vain of my size just then—
     A boy, as you might say,
Who takes to aping the ways of men,
     And home for the holiday.
Oh the dear old home, with its lighted hall,
     And windows all aglow,
And the holly wreaths on the parlor wall—
      Heigho!

My father welcomed many a guest
   To the Christmas carnival,
But cousin Maud, in her white robes dressed,
   Was fairest of them all ;
Oh, the deep alcove, and the window seat,
   And the blue eyes lifted there;
And the face that turned, with a cheek that
      burned,
   From a boy's too eager prayer !
Ah well !—the sigh of life drifts by,
   The taper of hope burns low,
But the ashy stain of its fires remain—
      Heigho !

Oh, the life we seek and the life we win
Are wide apart, but I deem it sin
   To waste warm breath in sighs,
We must drink the draught, tho' it be not
      sweet;
We must tread the path, tho' it wound our
      feet;
What we can not shun let us bravely meet;
   Life's bitterest moment flies.
That old love vow is a memory now—
   I married ?—yes, years ago.

That one so bright on the Christmas night?
          No, no !
There are joys too sweet for the heart to
          meet,
    I think, in its path below;
Earth would be heaven, if too complete—
          Heigho !

In the old home hall was a carnival,
    Again on a Christmas night;
And the holly wreaths on the parlor wall
    Glistened in rays as bright;
And brows of beauty, and eyes of mirth,
Braided a wreath for the Christmas hearth.
And there fell no tear for the blighted flowers,
Shrouded so cold in their ruined bowers;
And there breathed no sigh for the lost of
          ours,
    Missed from the festive hall.
But a boy with an ashy lip stood there,
And coldly looked on the brows most fair,
For his dumb thought clung in its mad de-
          spair .
    To the flowers neath their snowy pall ;
For cousin Maud, in her white robes dressed,
    Was fairest of them all.

SORROW.

BY SARAH E. CARMICHAEL.

THERE are many tones of sorrow,
 But its saddest voice to me,
Is the mocking laugh that triumphs
 In another's agony;
I could weep for those that suffer,
 But the souls that woe can please—
Whose joy is wrung from others' pain—
 I pity, *pity* these.

There are many tones of sorrow,
 Poured upon the chords of life,
Murmurs of its ceaseless changing,
 Murmurs of its restless strife;
But to live till pity's pleading
 Changes to a mocking hiss,
Till feeling withers to a sneer,
 Oh, Father, spare me this.

THE GOBLIN TAPESTRY.

BY MAY WENTWORTH.

'NEATH the eaves there sits a goblin,
  In the sunshine and the rain,
Dreamily the wooing south wind
  Whispers in his ear in vain.

Through the spring, all light and beauty,
  And the flush of summer time,
Through the mellow haze of autumn,
  And the winter's glittering rime.

E'en when chilling storms are raging,
  And the bitter north winds blow,
And the heavy clouds are bending
  To the earth, o'ercharged with snow.

When the dying boughs are creaking
  O'er the shattered window-pane,
And the maddened sea is wailing
  In a fitful, wild refrain.

Still beneath the eaves the goblin
   Sits, unmindful of the strife,
Weaving with untiring fingers
   The strange warp and woof of life.

In that tapestry are mingled
   Varied scenes of light and shade,
Woven in undying colors
   Neither sun nor dew can fade.

Oft the warp of hope is blended
   With the woof of dark despair,
And the cords of joy and sorrow
   Oft are twined together there.

There the secrets most we cherish,
   Which would cause the blush of shame,
Oft are traced 'mid golden pictures
   Twined with laurel wreaths of fame.

Curious tapestry, enwoven
   By the goblin of the eaves,
Picturing all life's waste and stubble,
   All its rich and garnered sheaves.

Never will the goblin weary,
    Till through shadows, the cold hand
Of the spectre death shall lead us
    To the unknown spirit land.

THE TWO WORLDS OF THE POET.

BY MAY WENTWORTH.

In two worlds the poet dwelleth,
  One, the never-changing real,
With its dull and dreary routine,
  One, the beautiful ideal.

Oh! the rapturous ideal!
  Rare, luxurious and bright,
Is the dream-land, radiant dream-land,
  Bathed in seas of mellow light.

There the streamlets flow in measures,
  Breathing soft, delicious rhyme,
And the wild flowers blush and linger,
  Fearless of the hand of time.

There the birds of pleasant spring-time
  Greet the poet with a song,
While responsive in his bosom
  Echoes sweet the notes prolong.

And the gorgeous tints of autumn
  Paint themselves upon his brain,
Till their richness gathering round him
  Never leaves his soul again.

And then come those forms of beauty,
  Visions radiant, dreams of love,
Till the bliss of heaven, the golden,
  Falls upon him from above.

And they woo the poet's spirit,
  Woo it by their magic art,
Born of mystery and enchantment,
  Beauty lives within its heart.

Thus the poet ever dwelleth
  In two worlds—one is the real,
With its dull and changeless routine,
  One, the beautiful ideal.

MISSING AND LOST.

EXTRACT FROM THE NORTHERN SEER.

"Missing and Lost!" "Missing and Lost!"
 The evening papers read.
Thus a young girl pale, with a sad heart wail,
 Looked over the list of the dead:
Looked over the list of the dead! not there
 Was the name she feared to see.
But missing and lost! Missing and lost!
 Oh! *Where could the missing be?*

The night-wind's wail swept over the vale,
 And entered the poor girl's heart—
Ah! a bitter pain was the sad refrain,
 It made her shrink and start.
A haunting fear was drawing near,
 A cold and chilling dread—
What if "missing and lost! missing and
 lost!"
 Should mean *alone* and *dead!*

But no one could tell what bitterness fell,
 "Missing and lost!" could mean.
She must wait, and wait—oh! wretched fate,
 The unknown! the unseen!

And her poor heart must bound and start
  At a foot-fall on the stair,
The step gone by, then drooping lie
  Down in her deep despair.

On the window-pane the beating rain
  Tolled like a funeral knell,
But "missing and lost! missing and lost!"
  Was all the tale it could tell.
And the dismal chime, in the dark night's
    time,
  Wailed the same pityful strain.
"The missing are where? God pity us,
    where?"
  Was ever the wild refrain.

Her poor fevered brain was burning with
    pain—
  "Ah! me!" she wretchedly said—
"Ah! how can I wait, to know his sad fate?
  Would to God, I were dead!"
Oh! the bitterest woe is not to know
  What missing, this missing, can mean,
Oh! madness is fed by such torturing dread
  Of the terrible, the unseen.

Still came the rain on the window-pane,
   And still the night-wind's wail—
"Missing and lost! missing and lost!"
   It said to the maiden pale;
And her heart's deep pain echoed the strain—
   "Missing." Ah! what can it mean?
Better be dead than wait and dread
   The unknown, the unseen!

15

NEW YEAR'S EVE.

BY CLARA CLYDE.

PUT by thy weary work, wife,
    And come and sit by me;
And we will talk of dear old times
    And our old home by the sea.
Oh, wipe away your tears, wife,
    We surely need not grieve
That the old, old year will die
    This bonnie New Year's Eve.

It brought us many griefs, wife,
    Though sent they were by God;
It saw us lay our boy to sleep
    Beneath the foreign sod;
It knew us in our own land, wife,
    Whose shores it saw us leave;
Alack! we'd better, better smile
    Than weep this New Year's Eve.

It has seen warm hearts grow chill, wife,
    And kindly hands grow cold;
But we'll look forth to the New Year,
    And not back to the old.

We'll thank our gracious God, wife,
    For gifts we may receive,
We'll thank God for his blessings,
    This bonnie New Year's Eve.

The night is cold and clear, wife,
    And youthful cheeks are red;
The Old Year lays his trembling hands,
    Upon each bended head.
Ah, well! we sit by our quiet fire,
    And never think to grieve
That younger hearts will gladder be
    This bonnie New Year's Eve.

NO BABY IN THE HOUSE.

BY CLARA CLYDE.

No baby in the house, I know—
    'Tis far too nice and clean;
No toys by careless fingers strewn
    Upon the floors are seen.
No finger-marks are on the panes,
    No scratches on the chairs,
No wooden men set up in rows,
    Or marshaled off in pairs;
No little stockings to be darned,
    All ragged at the toes,
No pile of mending to be done,
    Made up of baby clothes;
No little troubles to be soothed,
    No little hands to fold,
No grimy fingers to be washed,
    No stories to be told;
No tender kisses to be given,
    No nick-names—" Clove " and
        " Mouse ";
No merry frolics after tea—
    No baby in the house.

THREE AND TWO.

BY CLARA CLYDE.

As I passed along the shady lane,
  Twixt the meadow-land and wood,
I saw a blossom neath my feet—
  "Three Faces Under a Hood."

The maidens call it Heart's-ease—
  A name both sweet and good—
But best I like its country name,
  "Three Faces Under a Hood."

Then I passed along yet farther,
  In a careless, happy mood,
And I saw, 'neath a drooping grape-vine,
  Two Faces under a Hood.

Ah! one was dark and manly,
  And one was sweet, I ween;
And well they went together,
  Twenty and seventeen.

I looked at them, and my foolish eyes
   Grew very, very wet;
And my heart went back to my youthful
      days,
   Too beautiful to forget.

FRAGMENT FROM AN UNFINISHED POEM.

BY INA D. COOLBRITH.

OH, balm, and dew, and fragrance of those
    nights
Of Southern splendor 'neath a Southern sky!
The soft star-closes to the golden days
I dreamed away, in that far, tropic clime,
Wherein Love's blossom budded, bloomed
    and died!
How many arrows from Time's quiver fell
Around us, love, unheeded! while we roamed
Through fruited avenues of odorous limes,
Of citron and banana—where the air
Seemed swooning with its weight of rifled
    sweets.
Or down the spectral glen, where the black
    stream
Over the jagged gashes of gray rock
Whirled shriekingly—and the close air seemed
    filled
With viewless phantoms of accursed things.
We, wandering, found a weird magnificence

Even amid its horrors; for we clothed
Each dim surrounding object, with the hues
Of our own worship—and the things that else
Had seemed most darksome and unlovely,
    were,
By our great love, transfigured to divine.
Rose-shadowed, in the dreamy silences,
What long, long hours we paced the orient
    vale,
Robed in its Eden-splendor of rich bloom!
The amber moon hung low i' the mid-heaven;
Long, crimson blossoms of pomegranate
    boughs
Swung, censor-like, above us; and we saw,
Afar in the dim south, the long, sharp line
Of castellated rocks, keen-piercing through
The silver-veined tissues of the night:
We caught blue glimpses of the hills beyond;
And like a diamond set in the cleft heart
Of an emerald, the tiny lake shone out,
Its clear, unshadowed crystal mirroring
A·sky aflame with stars. We heard the low,
Soft plashing of the waves against the shore;
And caught snow-gleamings of an odorous
    weight
Of milk-white lilies, stirred by the slow tide.

LOVE IN LITTLE.

BY INA D. COOLBRITH.

BECAUSE the rose the Bloom of Blossoms is,
    And queenliest in beauty and in grace,
The violet's tender blue we love no less,
    Or daisy, glancing up with shy, sweet face.

For all the music which the forest has—
    The ocean-waves that crash upon the beach,
Still would we miss the whisper of the
        grass,
    The hum of bees, the brooklet's silver
        speech.

We would not have the timid wood-thrush
        mute,
    Because the bulbul more divinely sings;
Or lose the scarlet of dear Robin's throat
    For all the Tropics' flash of golden wings.

So do I think, though weak we be and small,
    Yet is there One whose care is none the less,
Who finds, perchance, some grain of worth
        in all,
    Or loves us for our very humbleness.
        15*

SUNSÉT.

BY INA D. COOLBRITH.

ALONG yon purple rim of hills,
How bright the sunset glory lies!
Its radiance spans the western skies,
    And all the slumbrous valley fills:

Broad shafts of lurid crimson, blent
With lustrous pearl in massed white;
And one great spear of amber light
    That flames o'er half the firmament!

Vague, murmurous sounds the breezes
        bear;
A thousand subtle breaths of balm,
From some far isle of tropic calm,
    Are borne upon the tranced air.

And, muffling all its giant-roar,
The restless waste of waters, rolled
To one broad sea of liquid gold,
    Goes singing up the shining shore!

OUT THROUGH THE GOLDEN GATE.

BY INGLE.

FAR out, in the dim and the dark of the
    waves
  That have gone through the Golden Gate,
Chanting a requiem over the graves
Of sailors who sleep in the coral caves,
    My thoughts are wafted by fate—
          Sad thoughts!
  Wafted out through the Golden Gate.

Far over the rolling ocean-hill,
  O'er the hill where the white ships go,
I see the barks that are rolling; and still
My thoughts go out far o'er the hill,
    While my heart is aching so—
          Ah, heart!
  While the white ships come and go.

All around me is very fair; and, oh!
  There is much in life to love!
Yet—strange that my dreams should wander
    so

Over the hills where the white ships go—
　Why do they ever rove?
　　　　　Sweet dreams,
　Ah, truants that ever rove!

Oh! wandering thoughts and fairy-like
　dreams,
　Ever roving against my will,
What star do you see? has it fairy beams
To lure you away o'er the ocean streams,
　Ah, heart that is wandering still!
　　　　　Truant heart!
　Far over the ocean-hill!

SUNSET.

BY INGLE.

The mountains stand,
Clearly defined—against the blood-red sky:
The waves, retreating from the rocky strand
Into the mist and gloom, go hand in hand,
　　　To sob and die.

The night comes on,
Trailing toward the west her dusky robe:
One bright star sits in beauty, all alone,
Upon the brow of night, as on a throne,
　　　Queen of the globe.

In such a light,
So filled with glory, let me ever lie:
With mountains, sunset, and the gloom of
　　night,
The waves retreating, till they seem to smite
　　　The blood-red sky.

THERE WAS A SHIP WENT OUT TO SEA.

BY JEAN BRUCE WASHBURN.

THERE was a ship went out to sea,
And it bore my love away—
My love with glossy dark brown hair,
And eyes of the thoughtful gray.
The birds may sing
Of the happy Spring,
But my heart can find no May.

Sunshine danced at the vessel's prow,
As my love went out to sea;
Lilies bloomed on the reedy shore,
And shook 'neath the humming bee.
The birds may sing
Of the happy spring,
No charm hath the Spring for me.

Linnets were building beneath our porch,
Like nuns in the limber grass;
The crickets sang to cheer that morn,
A tender farewell mass;

While from my sight,
Like form of light,
I saw my loved one pass.

Oh! how can the human heart be gay,
    When its sun of hope hath set?
And how can the lips that loved us once
    All coldly say, forget?
        The birds may sing,
        But for me the Spring
    Is the graveyard of regret.

For as that ship with its iron wheels
    Furrowed the golden sea,
It seemed some monster, huge and stern,
    That sneered at my misery.
        The birds may sing
        Of the happy Spring,
    But life has no Spring for me.

A SONNET:

ON McDONALD CLARKE'S UNREQUITED LOVE.

BY JEAN BRUCE WASHBURN.

"Sweet Mary, are we parted?   Oh! 'twas hard to part
    With the only blessing life had ever known,
To bear about the world an aching heart,
    And in the midst of millions be alone."
                                        McDONALD CLARKE.

To dream of thee through time's care-shad-
        ow'd hours,
    To worship thee, yet hope for no return;
To nurse love's corpse in mem'ry's faded
        bowers,
    And bend in tears o'er Hope's cold funeral
        urn!
To hear glad voices thrilling through the air,
    To feel thy heart responding with a moan,
To have thy steps tracked by Want's fiend,
        Despair—
    And 'mid earth's multitudes to pine alone;
To see all smiling, and to look in vain
    For one kind glance or tone to cheer thy
        lot;

To pass through showers of disappointment's
      rain!
  See others lov'd and be thyself forgot.
Such was his fate who wrote this sombre verse;
Poor broken heart! Death was thy kindest
      nurse.

BLUSHING.

BY FANNIE BRUCE COOK.

LOVELIEST by far is beauty's cheek
  When tinged with the crimson hue;
The delicate tints a soul that speak,
  Kind, innocent and true.
A word or look may start the stream,
  From heart to temples rushing;
Who loves not the modest face to view,
  Suffused in artless blushing?

Pure token thou of a sinless breast,
  Where kindliest virtues dwell,
Where truth and peace like angels rest,
  And wreathe their holiest spell;
Slight the emotion that stirs the tide,
  The brow of candor flushing;
Oh! the gentlest feelings of the heart
  Are told in artless blushing.

The gem may add its lustrous ray
  To adorn the outward part,
But the changeful hues of the blush's play
  Are the language of the heart;

For they tell of a mind undimm'd by vice,
    All spell of evil hushing;
O, who would e'er doubt the guileless soul
    That speaks in artless blushing?

The colorless face, the pallid brow,
    May perhaps enchant thine eye,
But give me the cheek that owns the glow
    Of nature's healthful dye.
It seems to shadow an honest mind,
    Where purest thoughts are gushing,
And loveliest far is beauty's cheek,
    When tinged with artless blushing.

THE NEW YEAR.

BY ISABEL A. SAXON.

ALL hail to thee, thou new-born heir of
    Time's eternal flight,
With varying hopes and promises prismat-
    ically bright,
With all thy wealth of future days, for sad-
    ness or for mirth—
Come as thou wilt, for weal or woe, we wel-
    come thee to earth!

Gay with the smiles of infancy, or saddened
    by the fears
Of Fate's untimeliest ministry, in wretched-
    ness and tears;
Come as the giver of delight, the herald of
    decay,
Thou still art welcome by a world of perish-
    able clay.

And yet what art thou but a mere imaginary
    span,
A link of Time's unending chain, as meas-
    ured out by man?

To youth a whole eternity—to age a phantom
    day,
To anxious hearts a weary time of trial and
    dismay.

Aye, new-born year, by hope enwreathed,
    how many aching hearts
Will cease from weariness and toil, ere thy
    brief life departs;
How many idols worshiped now will crum-
    ble into dust,
How many souls, too pure for earth, will
    mingle with the just!

The glorious and the beautiful, the eloquent
    and brave—
The free-born sons of Liberty—triumphant
    in the grave;
Genius, with her undying flame, hid like the
    stars away,
Merging in suns of purer light her own im-
    mortal ray.

Thou, too, wilt see the agony of much of
    earth's alloy,
Of sin, and shame and suffering—of sorrow
    as of joy.

The felon in his misery, the murderer in his
    cell,
Shall darkly turn amid thine hours from life
    and light to dwell.

Then, onward still.   As yet untrod, oh, may
    thy dim profound,
Gift of the God of victories, prove Free-
    dom's vantage ground !
And while the record of our lives is tracing
    on thy page,
Oh, may His smiles, who gave us thee, con-
    sole our pilgrimage.

THE VESTAL OF THE NIGHT.

BY ISABEL A. SAXON.

Oh, pure pale moon!
Wan Lady of the night,
Who, with mild beams so calmly sweet,
This worn and weary world dost greet
    With sympathetic light:
Art thou thus strangely pale
With watching o'er our human woe—
Mourning the never-ending tale of agony
        below?
Beneath thy gentle ray
    How many an aching heart
Hath wept its hour away,
    Now and in ages gone.
The captive chained afar,
    Aweary and alone—
The satrap on his gilded car
    A slave—upon a throne—
Thou hast beheld them all pass by
From thy silent home in the distant sky;
    And, many a time, too soon

Hast thou seen from the azure arch on
    high,
Earth's gifted ones depart.
Those of undying fame have been
Who gazed upon thee, beauteous queen,
    With rapture-kindling eye;
Gallileo, 'mid his prison bars,
So won his coronet of stars
    From Immortality.

    Oh, fair soft rays!
Still shining on as in long-gone days—
How o'er the earth-worn soul
Ye fling the sense of a pure control
    From lovelier worlds than this;
What holy mysteries hover round,
Making, 'mid things of sense and sound,
    A paradise of bliss!
Silent and smooth on the glassy tide
    Your lingering glories play,
    Shedding on dusky night—
Thus gem-adorned like an Orient bride—
    A softened gleam of eternal day,
    With heaven's own brilliance bright;
So, by Death's chastening hand,

Shall the dull dark load of this mortal clay
   Be changed to immortal light
On the shore of the Radiant Land.

  ·   Vestal of altars high,
   Bearing the sacred flame,
Reflected back through the starry sky,
   Which from God's great Presence came,
We kneel—we know not why—
   'Mid our toil of strife and tears,
With a yearning trust in the hopes that lie
   Hid in the far off spheres,
And a faith in the immortality
   Of never-ending years—
When life's long warfare o'er,
   Earth's changeful journey done—
We shall drag the cross and chain no more
   In our nightly orison,
But shall scan the page of celestial lore
   With the crown of knowledge won.

16

BYRON.

BY MRS. V. E. HOWARD.

"UNFOUND the boon, unslaked the thirst"—
    Alas!
He did the crystal, bubbling well o'erpass
To quench his thirst within the dark morass;
Turning from love's pure spring, he sunk
    his soul
In passion's tide, whose waves tumultuous
    roll.

Yet often sparkled forth a purer ray,
And what he might have been—Ah! who
    can say?
For surely he was nature's finer clay,
And his soul pined for higher—nobler aim,
But error still her votary will claim.

And when the eagle did his flight essay,
Unblenchingly toward the source of day,
He found his fettered pinions useless lay,
For he had "filled his soul" and could no
    more
Unclogged unto the bright empyrean soar.

In Greece he died—died even in his prime,
Afar from all of error or of crime,
From all that heretofore had stained his time;
Working in Freedom's cause the *poet* died,
Oh! who can tell what name was his beside.

Had he then lived, perchance had that name,
Gleaming with lustre wild, a meteor flame,
Redeemed and set amid the stars of fame;
'Tis useless to reflect what might have been,
And yet we still must grieve he perished then.

For when still young—a gifted soul has fled;
We seem to bury in the funeral bed
The *future promise*, with the early dead;
For none can do, that breathe beneath the
    sun,
The mind-work that another left undone;
The race is finished—but the goal *unwon*.

THE GENIUS OF AMERICAN LIBERTY.

BY FANNY G. M'DOUGAL.

SHE sat on the mast of the Mayflower,
  She perched in the white, wintry wood,
And as the brave barque bore inland
  On a crag of the cliff she stood;
And she heard the Pilgrim's pæan
    Over the wild waves roll,
"We build in the forest a temple,
    To Liberty of Soul!"
And waving wood and heaving main,
Sang, answering to the bold refrain,
    "To Liberty of Soul!"

She stood on the summit of Bunker
  When the storm of battle awoke,
And the shock of the thundering cannon
  From the cloud of the onset broke;
And she cried, with a din that sounded
    Above the battle's breath,
"Press on, ye noble Warriors!
    To victory, or death!"

Then sharply rang the clashing steel
With arm-ed hoof, and arm-ed heel,
  "To victory, or death!"

She stooped in the cloud over Yorktown,
  When the foes of Freedom failed,
And before our glorious Leader
  The brave Cornwallis paled;
And she heard in the boom of the ocean,
    In the song of the woodland bowers,
And the breath of the rock-ribbed moun-
      tains,
  "Freedom for us and ours!"
Then high her starry banner swung,
And far the victors' chorus rung,
  "Freedom for us, and ours!"

She stood by the marbled Hero,
  When the damning deed was done,
And the Friends of Right were gathered
  In the shadow of Washington;
And she heard the serried City
    To the distant cities call,
"Up, with your mail-ed millions,
    Up for the Union! all!"

Then rolled along the distant sky
A pealing, pealing, pealing cry,
  "For Union stand, or fall!"

They came with the tread of an earthquake,
  The ground beneath them shook;
And the loyal thought, and the loyal word,
  To their heart of hearts they took;
And who shall stand before them,
    Or break their God-armed van,
Who go forth but to conquer
    For Freedom, and for man!
Then lift our time-worn banner high,
And wake our ancient battle cry;
  "For Freedom, and for Man!"

Press on, ye glorious Freemen!
  Bear down the craven band!
For home, for wives and children,
  Freedom and Native Land!
Keep every soldier's honor,
    As gleaming sabre bright,
And cut each clanking fetter
    With the tempered blade of Right;
On, with stout heart, and straining breath,
For Freedom, Victory, or Death!
    Charge home! charge heavy! charge!

"THEO"—AGED FIFTEEN.

BY MRS. JAMES NEALL.

THE while I listened to the sounding glory
　　　　Of the far reaching sea,
A mother's lips were telling the sweet story
　　　　Of Theo unto me.
The tender, solemn story of sweet Theo
　　unto me.

How all her life was rounded into beauty,
　　　　And passing days,
But saw her treading higher slopes of beauty,
　　　　And gladder ways;
And how her spring-time blossomed 'neath
　　the rays

Of love, which made an azure of her heaven,
　　　　And round her threw
Soft shadows such as glorify at even
　　　　· The drifting blue,
When dying sunlight sends spent arrows
　　through.

And all the while the day was slowly paling
Away from sight,
Yet on the sky, a gold and sapphire railing
Barred out the night,
And mellowing twilight purpled all the light.

A sweet, sad story—sweet in that recalling
Beside the sea,
It seemed as though a lovely star was falling
Away from me,
A star, whose unseen, trackless path was all
eternity.

For THEO DIED! Alas! the mournful mean-
ing
Athwart my soul,
Fell like a shadow over all things leaning,
And dirge and dole
Thenceforth were surging in the wild waves'
roll.

And thus methought—Life is a flickering
taper,
And Death may come,
To quench its flame, as a mephitic vapor;
Then cold and numb,
In the drear darkness, Hope itself sits dumb.

Nay some sweet spirit whispered, as the
    glory
        Of the far reaching sea,
Became a requiem and memento mori,
        Of Theo unto me;
God early sets his chosen angels free.

And she was gathered, a sweet odored blos-
    som,
        While yet the dew
Was lying like a pearl upon her bosom,
        And all the Blue,
Perpetual sunlight round about her threw.

Would ye have kept her till the winds had
    rifted,
        The bud apart?
And one by one the tender leaves had drifted,
        Leaving her heart
Bare and unsheltered for the Archer's dart?

Ye know not now—ye may not hear the
    singing
        Of glad release,
How Death, the white winged, unto her was
    bringing,

16*

The boon of peace,
Your lamb was folded with unspotted fleece.

Oh! father! mother! well I know the weep-
        ing
        Beneath the smile,
The tender memories that your hearts are
        keeping;
        How all the while
Ye whisper each to each—so pure, so free
        from guile.

Why could it be?   Oh! God's mysterious
        dealing
        Ye may not scan,
But *all* is ordered the redemption sealing,
        Of fallen man;
And life and death are wheels to carry on
        His plan.

Then rest in this—the silent inward teaching
        E'en while ye weep,
And ever as your thoughts are upward reach-
        ing,
        The memory keep
Of that sweet psalm; "God giveth His *be-
loved*, sleep."

APRIL AND MAY.

BY MARGARET A. BROOKS.

SWEET April wept, while bright May slept,
And soft I heard her say—
"Not thine the care, what thou shall wear,
On coronation day;
Sleep, sister, sleep, and I will keep
Bright watch o'er leaf and flower;
For thee I'll woo the pearly dew,
The soft and genial shower."

Then soon was heard, the song of bird,
And buds wreathed every bough,
When in May's bower, at midnight hour,
She whispered, "Wake thee now."—
But happy May unconcious lay
In Spring's warm, sheltering breast;
Sweet April smiled, and round the child
A rosy mantle pressed.

She kissed her cheek, and scarce could speak,
But breathed with tender sigh—
"Oh, lovely May, I must not stay,
Good bye, my love, good bye."

She soared on high through dappled sky,
And ne'er again was seen;
At dawn of day, woke beauteous May,
And found herself—a queen.

LIGHT.

BY MRS. P. A. ROGERS.

Where the tiny dew-drop shineth,
  On the radiant brow of morn;
Where a sheen of silver, lineth
  Heaven's blue arch, at early dawn;

Where the sunbeams flash and quiver,
  On the azure ocean's breast;
Where the bosom of the river
  Smiles in gladness, there I rest.

Where the fleecy clouds are sailing
  Over heaven's majestic plain;
Where the starbeams, never failing,
  Fall in showers of silver rain;

Where the bow of promise, lingers,
  With its many colored dyes;
There I point, with rosy fingers,
  To my home beyond the skies.

THE APPLE WOMAN'S STORY.

BY MRS. J. M. SANDERS.

"WILL you buy an apple, madame?—here's
 a pippin bright as gold,
Better never ripened—and many a fine one I
 have sold:—
Here's red and russet, less beautiful, but just
 as sound and sweet.
Thank you, lady; little Miss has chosen well
 her luscious treat.

"How it warms my heart to see her beaming
 face, so pure and mild;
'Tis a glimpse of heaven—the darling! be
 not afraid of me, fair child;
Though I am like the sear and blasted tree,
 it was not always so,
I once was ruddy, and blithe, and strong,—a
 long, long time ago.

"And I am so accustomed to it now, I quite
 forget the shame
Of my scars and crooked limbs—true, misfortune is no blame.

I have never looked upon a glass, since I
    learned to look within,
And face the ugliness found. there—for who
    is free from sin?

"Yes, I am growing old, dear lady, shall be
    sixty-nine to morrow;
I have had sore trials in my time, too; heaps
    upon heaps of sorrow.
Yet I don't repine; there's nothing now can
    ever grieve me more,
And I am thankful I have not to beg my
    bread from door to door.

"Tell you about it?—yes, I will: 'tis a dreary
    tale of woe,
That now seems like a troubled dream, it
    happened so long ago.
You can scarce believe, my dear, that I was
    once a pretty girl,
With eyes as bright and blue as yours, and
    many a golden curl.

"I was a loved and happy child, though
    reared on coarsest food,
And my home the humblest cottage that with-
    out our village stood.

No lighter step than mine was seen, no mer-
    rier voice was heard,
In the meadows where I tossed the hay, and
    caroled like a bird.

"I had many suitors, and might have married
    better, to be sure;
Yet I was rich in Harry's love—fond hearts
    are never poor.
Father and mother—they had only me—I
    left for him I chose,
And parting was my heart's first grief; but
    so the holy mandate goes.

"Folks said we were a handsome pair; a
    proud and joyous wife,
I little thought life's thorny path led through
    darkness, tears and strife.
We left the village for the town, for the sake
    of Harry's trade;
—A ship-carpenter, my dear—and a good
    livelihood he made.

"Snugly and happily we lived, as small com-
    forts round us grew;
A blessing rested on us then, and twice a
    mother's joy I knew.

The cunning ways of baby, the prattle of our
    chubby lad,
A tidy hearth, and cheerful smiles, made the
    home-welcome glad.

"One evening, keeping holiday, we went to
    see the play,
And left our blooming little Rose with a
    neighbor, on the way.
Ann had a nursling of her own, there seemed
    no reason for regret,
Yet I had misgivings—and my lips with
    baby's tears were wet.

"I wearied of the mirth and glare, and at
    Nature's mute demand,
More than once my tingling bosom seemed
    to feel her playful hand.
Like one entranced I sat, save that I shud-
    dered as with fear,
And dismal sounds, like those of pain, mur-
    mured faintly on my ear.

"The curtain fell—we hurried out—then like
    a surging ocean,
The clang of bells—the cry of 'FIRE,' the
    engines' rushing motion,

Swelled louder as we neared our home, light-
    ed by lurid flashes,
Alas! to find a smoking ruin—a heap of
    smoldering ashes.

"Shielding our boy, my husband parted from
    me, pressed along;
But I thought only of my babe, and pierced
    the laboring throng.
Unmindful of the fiery rain,—oh, 'twas like
    the Day of Doom!
I gained the burning house, and rushed up
    stairs to Annie's room.

"Dizzied and blind, a feeble wail my stag-
    gering footsteps led,
To snatch a muffled infant from the floor—I
    would have fled,
Great God! the stairs had disappeared; and
    roaring tongues of flame,
Mingled with hissing streams and stifling
    gusts, toward me fiercely came.

"A cry of horror from the crowd answered
    my tortured scream,
When at the casement, framed in fire, my
    pleading form was seen;

And daring arms were stretched to save the
    little life I did implore;
I sprang—as 'twere into a blazing gulf—and
    knew no more.

"The ways of Providence are dark to us;
    strange, and past finding out;
Oh, in my grief and pain I dared awhile their
    justice doubt.
I left the hospital a hideous thing—helpless
    and lame:
And 'twas *Annie's baby I had saved—mine per-
ished in the flame.*

"—She was rescued, Madam, from above, at
    the bedside of her boys,
Their youthful sleep, unconscious, alike of
    peril and of noise.
Want is selfish—yet Ann was true to me,
    though a poor sailor's wife;
Good soul! she would insist she'd been to
    blame, and thought so all her life.

"Though health returned, each passing day
    saw some fresh joy or hope depart;
For Harry never was the same, he took our
    losses so to heart:

Moody or wild, neglecting work, he sought
    the tavern's hateful spell,
Ah, guess what followed—*his shame* is not for
    my poor tongue to tell.

"I struggled on, early and late toiled, more
    than my strength could bear,
Though Charlie's little gains were proudly
    brought for me to share.
Then happened—what I had long foreseen—·
    after years of silent woe;
Yet the tears of *widowhood* came with a bit-
    ter, bitter flow.

"And lonely were the hours I passed, while
    Charlie was at sea,
He was a wondrous clever lad—and so dutiful
    to me!
I know not how he learned it all—with what
    a sunny smile,
He'd tell his jokes and marvelous long yarns
    our evenings to beguile.

"Well—a dreadful winter came; food was
    dear, 'twas bitter cold, beside;
Many a poor wretch went supperless, many
    a famished infant died.

I counted every lengthened day, as a miser
    counts his store,
For with the buds of Spring would come my
    darling to my arms once more.

"I remember how I used to sit and watch
    the little star,
He told me guided mariners, wandering on
    seas afar;
And how my yearning heart went out, as I
    walked at eve alone,
Beside the restless ocean, saddened by its sol-
    emn moan.

"And oh, I never shall forget, when the great
    storm began,
How the wind howled at the shivered pane,
    and the rain in torrents ran;
How I held my fainting breath, at the awful
    thunder of the deep,
And all night long I wept and prayed, and
    never thought of sleep.

"And what a mortal dread I felt, when cow-
    ering at the hearth,
An icy kiss upon my brow, left a farewell,
    not of earth.

A sudden stillness fell at morn, and when I
    looked upon the street,
The white snow lay in drifted folds, like a
    glistening winding-sheet.

"Three days, three fearful days, the tempest
    raged before 'twas truly known,
How, while saving other lives, my noble boy
    had lost his own;
And almost in sight of home, the stately ship
    had gone ashore,
Freighted with precious souls, whose little
    dream of earth was o'er.

"Small comfort was it to me then to hear his
    frozen corse was found,
And with others decently interred in conse-
    crated ground;
But now I'm glad to know he sleeps beneath
    the heaven's blue pall,
With a sunny sod upon his breast, where
    summer roses fall.

"You weep—aye, so did I, in those sad times,
    until my heart was dry;
But now I'm waiting patiently to join them
    all on high.

I have earned a pittance, just enough a pau-
 er's end to save—
And have a spotless suit laid by, to clothe
 me for the grave.

"I can not see through it at all, yet I *feel*
 that God is good,
That His sacred promises are kept, though
 not always understood.
No kindred branch is left me, but he has lent
 a little flower,
To cheer my wintry age, and dew with tears
 its last dark hour.

"'Tis Nellie, Madam, Annie's grandchild,
 now orphaned and alone,
I love the dear good girl, and oftentimes
 forget she's not my own.
On holidays, and the brief hours that labor
 leaves to spare,
She never fails to come and soothe me with
 many a tender care.

"Together then we gossip, and the pleasant
 time flies fast,
While she prophecies the future, and I preach
 about the past.

And that is all my story, dear.   When the
    weather is not too cold,
You'll find me hereabouts—not long, though,
    for I'm waxing weak and old."

THE TWO HOMES.

BY MRS. CHAS. B. HOPKINS.

LAND of the West, the soft South-West,
　　Whose winters are all Junes;
Where weary-footed pride may rest,
And hearts by empty forms opprest,
　　May beat their own wild tunes.

Land where the laborer goes his way,
　　Imperial as a king,
At morning, though a knoll of clay
Have been his pillow where he lay,
　　His blanket, night's dark wing.

Land where the sack received the grain
　　Fresh from the reaper's flail;
Nor needs a barn o'er all the plain,
With graceless roof to shed the rain,
　　And meet the pelting hail.

Land of the gold, the silver bed,
　　Land of the copper mines;

17

Where modest beauty haply wed,
Smiles sweetly in the lowliest shed
    That nestles in the vines.

Land where centurial cedars tower,
    The poet's true ideal;
Where snow-cliffs hang o'er vales in flower,
And birds, alike in sun or shower,
    Sing on with joyous peal.

A pilgrim to thy shores I come,
    Thou earthly better land;
For winter chilled me sore at home,
The ice-dew touched my brow with foam,
    And froze on every hand.

The home resigned was sweet and dear,
    "On Susquehanna's side,
Fair Wyoming!" the last, last tear
I've dropped upon thy river clear,
    Old Pennsylvania's pride.

Home that I loved—ye friends behind,
    One earnest, long adieu!
As holy relics borne in mind,
Your pictures in my bosom shrined
    Are lettered, "tried and true."

Farewell! through wastes of distance now,
   I gaze with eyes astrain;
O'er billowy years that ebb and flow,
Sweet voices of the Long Ago,
   Sound soft as dripping rain.

But yet I feel the potent charm
   Of this more genial shore;
The plow upturns the furrow warm,
'Mid January's sun and storm
   We sit with open door.

My home is where the fig tree yields
   Her fruit, no bloom astart;
But, night to all *one* heaven reveals,
Our varied paths one Father shields,
   And clasps us to His heart.

.

A FIRESIDE PICTURE.

BY MRS. L. NORTON.

I OFTEN hear a song at night,
When the darkling windows are curtained
    tight,
And lamp and fire are burning bright.

These marshaled their flames an hour ago,
And charged, with their weapons all aglow,
The shadows, and routed them high and low.

Our mother, dear lady! is on the wall,
Held there by a paint and canvass thrall,
But her eyes beam love upon us all.

Our all is two—my husband and I ;
As eventide is drawing nigh,
He dons a robe of richest dye.

Its folds with a silken cord are bound,
And here and there, on its crimson ground,
Leaves of the palm and vine are found.

His comely feet are taking rest,
Each in a soft, embroidered nest,
Wrought by the fingers he loves best.

We are but two, yet not alone;
Friends, who into our love have grown,
Are all around us—all our own.

Obedient to our least command,
On table, shelf and desk they stand—
A quaint, mysterious, silent band.

They only speak at our desire,
But then they utter words of fire,
Or tune the poet's sweetest lyre.

My husband has found his easy chair;
I sit——but on his knee or where,
Of course is neither here nor there.

Soon from his firm and manly lips,
Ever hid in a deep eclipse
Of raven hair, sweet music slips.

Sweet, no doubt, to me alone;
No words nor air to call its own,
Nor artist skill, nor depth of tone.

But I, who listen every night,
And always with renewed delight,
Have learned to hear the song aright.

Mark, what it means: "Dear little wife,
Near thee, each hour with joy is rife;
Without thee, I should tire of life.

"Now I am happy, now I rest,
For thy dear head is on my breast,
Thy hand in mine is closely pressed.

"It seems to me that grief and gloom
Can never darken this cheerful room,
And wither away my darling's bloom."

What marvelous music could I hear
To bring such joy to my listening ear
As this, that has nightly grown so dear?

Dreaming thus, in the morning's prime,
I have wiled away the weary time,
In weaving together this idle rhyme.

THE FARMER AND THE MUSE.

BY AUDE VANE.

SWEET, sunny May, perfumed and gay,
   Peeps in at my door this morn,
A-wooing me, with songs of glee,
   To go—"and plant my corn."

O'er hills and streams sweet poet-dreams
   Are flitting to and fro;
No doubt some men would take the pen,
   But I—"shall take the hoe."

In woody bowers, the haunts of flowers,
   'Tis sweet to take one's ease;
I think each sight delicious, quite,
   And so—"are early peas."

The robin's song is sweet and long,
   And 'neath the porch the wrens
Are building nests; but I like best
   The—"cackling of the hens."

I never see on blushing tree
　　The apple blossoms hung,
But thoughts arise of "Autumn pies,"
　　And—"quartered apples strung."

I ne'er could see how men *could* be
　　So blind to Nature's charms,
When dales and hills, and sparkling rills
　　Compose—"such *splendid* farms."

Utility and Poetry
　　In this great age are growing;
"If I'd the say, to make things pay
　　I'd set the Muse to *hoeing*.

The wisest way, I'm free to say,
　　If *all* were of your notion;
For money's sake such men would make
　　A mill-pond of the ocean!

But some there be who love to see
　　The beauties of creation,
Without the bane of greedy gain,
　　Or thought of desecration.

The farmer deemed this wisdom gleamed
　　More purely bright than Plato's;
He hired the muse to state his views,
　　And paid her in—potatoes!

The cunning wight, thus fed to write,
　　Each verse to suit *him* ended,
But when "to grass" he sent the lass,
　　Her wrath in words descended.

"Ungrateful man," she said, "how can
　　You treat a lady badly?
You, like your wheat, are mixed with cheat,
　　And need a thrashing sadly.

"Like your own swine, you live to dine;
　　You starve your higher nature;
You may be sure *you'll* ne'er secure
　　My vote for legislature."

17*

FORBIDDEN FRUIT.

BY AUDE VANE.

In the garden of life's pleasures sure the tree
   is standing still—
Who can tell us if its fruitage yield us most
   of good or ill?
Only in the eating may we gain the knowledge of the Good;
Though the Evil may be bitter, can we help
   it if we would.

If upon each blushing apple unmistakably
   we saw,
"This thou shalt not eat, my children," then
   we might obey the law.
But, alas! the light of Eden from our eyes
   is banished far,
And each mortal holds his candle for his fellow's guiding star.

Still the lamp that is within us, lighted by
   the hand Divine,
Shineth for our special guidance, though all
   others cease to shine;

Yet our sight is often clouded, dimm'd by
    passing mote or beam,
And the fruit that looketh fairest, proveth
    not what it doth seem.

All may see and know their follies in the
    light the future brings,
But our present wisdom only shineth on the
    present things.
Should we blindly follow Custom? is he al-
    ways in the right?
Are the fruits he chooseth for us never
    spoiled by Evil's blight?

Aye! we know his cruel wine-press crusheth
    oft our grapes of joy,
'Till their wine, so harsh and bitter, sharpest
    appetites will cloy.
He, a blind and heartless tyrant, nourished
    by a selfish throng,
Led so oft by haughty Error—how can *he*
    be judge of wrong?

Ye who by your farthing rush-lights, view in
    gloom the deeds of all,
Turn you where, in purer regions, Charity's
    sweet light doth fall.

She will lead you in green pastures down be-
     side the waters still;
Let the love-light that she bringeth all your
     darksome corners fill.

She is kind in all her judgments, thinking
     evil thoughts of none;
Never making good for others that which
     pleaseth *her* alone;
Ne'er mistrusting or condemning all as wrong
     she cannot know,
For by many a hidden fountain purest fruits
     of pleasure grow.
Choose *her* then for your companion, by her
     light your judgment frame,
They who pluck the fruit forbidden, you by
     kindness may reclaim.

ROSEMARY.

BY MARY VIOLA TINGLEY.

INDIAN Summer has gone with its beautiful
moon,
And all the sweet roses I gathered in June
Are faded;—It may be the cloud-sylphs of
Even
Have stolen the tints of those roses for
Heaven.
O bonnie bright blossom! in the years far
away,
So evanished thy bloom on an evening in
May.

The sunlight now sleeps in the lap of the
west,
And the star-beams are barring its chamber
of rest,
While Twilight is weaving her blue-tinted
bowers
To mellow the landscape where slumber the
flowers.

I would fain learn the music that won thee
    away,
When the earth was the beautiful temple of
    May;
For our fancies were measured the bright
    summer long
To the carols we learned from the lark's
    morning song.
They still haunt me—those echoes from
    Child land—but now
My heart beats alone to their musical flow.

Then I never looked up to the portals on
    high,
For our Heaven was here; and our azure-
    stained sky
Was the violet mead; the cloud-billows of
    snow
Were the pale nodding lilies; the roses that
    glow
On the crown of the hill, gave the soft blush-
    ing hue;
The gold was the crocus; the silver, the dew
Which met as it fell, the glad sunlight of
    smiles,

And wove the gay rainbow of Hope, o'er our
    aisles.
But the charm of the spring-time has van-
    ished with thee;
To its mystical speech I've forgotten the
    key;
Yet, if angels and flowers *are* closely allied,
I may trace thy lost bloom on the blushing
    hillside;
And when rose-buds are opening their petals
    in June,
I'll feel thou art near me and teaching the
    tune
Which chanted by seraphim, won thee away
On that blossoming eve, from the gardens of
    May.

THE ARTIST'S GRAVE.

BY MRS. J. C. WINANS.

AH, this is Edward's grave. A narrow
    mound,
Just heaped above the cold and senseless
    ground,
With branches dry and sear wailing around.

Well! 'Twas fate. I loved him, or thought
    I did;
But then a wealthier suitor came, and bid
Higher for my hand, and I basely chid

Him away among the discarded rest,
And, marrying a titled man, became the guest
Of queens, matching my jewels with their
    best.

This morning one of the Court gossips said—
"The King's new protege, Edward Fay, is
    dead:
An artist rare, to paint and easel wed."

Dead a whole month!   I was ashamed to
    weep.
I wonder if, when last he fell asleep,
A woman's face bent o'er him, sad and sweet?

Dead!   Young Edward Fay mould'ring in a
    shroud!
Why, he was strong, and bore a heart too
    proud
To be crushed by nothing—a passing cloud!

He should have scorned me.   The world is
    wide.
He should have sought and found a fitter
    bride—
What matter?   Done anything, O, God!
    but died!

Dead!   And not a word of kind forgiveness
To lessen this weight of weary sadness.
I loved him.   To feel it now, is madness.

Who is to blame for this my loveless lot?
Myself did forge the chain around me dropt.
Myself—none other this agony begot.

Henceforth I am a gorgeous, jeweled slave.
And must wear smiles, a tyrant's heart to
    lave,
While mine is inly weeping o'er this grave:

Nay, ponder how to make my eyes dilate
With spurious joy, that no tongue may prate
Whether I bear my lord most love or hate.

So I must live forever with this thought,
That I, by love, the purest love was taught,
Then parted with it for the name I bought.

Yes, live! keeping my breaking heart engird
With mirth, to drop without toppling, light
    word
Whene'er my purchaser's light step is heard.

And so—farewell, dear Edward.   I am here—
Lady Vilna—(simple Laura last year)—
With eyes so hard they can not shed a tear.

O, Edward, would that I could weep or pray,
Or call thee back to life, and hear thee say,
"Thou art forgiven," ere I turn away.

Farewell! To-morrow—next day—forever—
To wear chains only death can sever—
To love, or be loved again, ah, never.

THE EMPTY STOCKING.

BY MRS. C. M. STOWE.

"O God!" the mother cried, as o'er her
    child
She leant, with loving eye, "and must I see
Thy little face, that looks so sweet and mild,
    Dreaming of morning, and the Christmas
      tree,
Look disappointed, and with wond'ring eyes
    Search in the stocking which must empty
      be?
Empty, because the hand that filled it lies
    Mouldering to dust beneath the sullen sea.

"One year ago thy little stocking hung
    Upon the self-same nail that holds it now,
Crowded so full of toys—thou art too young
    To read the sorrow written on my brow!
How can I tell thee, O, my little one!
    Thy father's with the angels in the sky,
And hear thy wond'ring questions, when I'm
      done,
    'If God is good, why did my papa die?'

"I watched thee on thy knees, my little boy,
   And heard thee mingling with thy childish
      prayer,
'And now I lay me—please, God, send me
      toys;
   Tell Santa Claus my stocking 's hanging
      there.'
Thy wants are few, thy heart is now at rest—
   The angels whisper to thee in thy sleep—
There are no presents, and my aching breast
   Yearns for the dead until I can but weep.

"I, too, have prayed, 'Give me this day our
      bread,'
   And like my little boy, no answer's given;
I can but mourn and wish that we were dead—
   Gone with our loved ones to the waiting
      heaven.
Oh! how that empty stocking mocks my
      prayer!
   My purse, too, empty, and the night half
      gone;
And just before me stands the vacant chair—
   All's cheerless save my little sleeping one.

"All, all is hopeless gloom—the windows
    creak,
  And night-winds whisper, faintly, through
    the room—
But, hark! I think I hear—O, Henry, speak!
  Art from the sky, or risen from the tomb?"
"My Mary, dear, I heard thy prayer to-
    night—
  The news was false, you see I am not dead;
Look, here are Willie's toys—give me the
    light—
  And Mary, dear, O, Mary, here is bread."

From that low roof another prayer went up,
  And all was answered in the morning light.
Stocking was full, and even Mary's cup
  Scarce held the blessings of the Christmas
    night.
Never a Christmas came more fraught with
    joy;
  Never were gifts more thankfully received;
Never was Mary prouder of her boy—
  Stocking was full—Willie was not deceived.

BIRDS IN THE CITY.

BY MRS. C. A. CHAMBERLAIN.

ROVERS of earth and air, why here abide?
Bright, blissful ones, how can you here find
    rest,
  Where little lovely is, and less is blest,
'Mid this vexed human tide?

  Why pour your sweet songs here amidst
    the din,
Unfettered ones, here where the fainting air
  Seems shrinking from the burden it must
    bear,
As conscience shrinks from sin?

  Nature has many places formed for you,
·Where ye may give your lays of love and
    bliss,
  Amidst a fairer, happier life than this,
'Midst sympathy most true.

Or seek the city haunted not by care—
The quiet city, where they strive no more,
    Your strains of life around the still ones
        pour—
Listeners may wait you there!

    Yet, if your song wins 'midst the thronged
        way
One brief, sad smile, that tells of other
        hours,
    The early home, and melody and flowers,
E'en for that smile's sake stay!

    Yet stay—if here one weary, aching breast,
That has of life but little save its wrong,
    Amidst its gloom, · is waiting for your
        song
To lull its woes to rest!

    Ye follow man where he a home doth
        find,
Pouring your music freely round his way,
    And ask not if he listens to the lay—
Thus should the poet mind.

Sing 'midst life's discord—sing for love's
    sweet sake,
Though few may seem to listen to the sound,
    The strains may play some weary heart
      around,
Hope's drooping flowers to wake.

18

"SUFFICIENT UNTO THE DAY IS THE EVIL THEREOF."—*Bible*.

BY E. LOUISE MILLS.

ONCE musing in my room I sat at the low
   midnight hour,
And memory of by-gone days rushed back
   with mighty power;
I thought of all the youthful hopes that in
   my path lay crushed,
I thought of all the music-chords that in my
   heart were hushed;
This earth that once an Eden seemed, now,
   sombre and uncouth,
Were not the semblance of the world I loved
   in early youth.

Ah, me! I cried, the rainbow bright that
   once my pathway spanned,
Hath fled away swift as the chaff by autumn's
   storm-wind fanned.
Oh the future! will it bring such feelings as
   the past?
Will hopes fill up the trembling heart, too
   beautiful to last?

Why are we thus in ignorance, why may we
    not behold
The wonderous scenes that lie beyond the
    veils mysterious fold?

Why should the future scenes, I said, be hid
    from mortal sight?
Rising up, I gazed around, when by my flick-
    ering light
I saw a white-robed being stand meekly be-
    fore my door,
A purer being than mine eyes had e'er beheld
    before;
He said, "your wishes unuttered hath an-
    swered been in heaven,
And to your inner light shall now a *single*
    glimpse be given."

He laid his hand upon my brow, and then
    with sudden fear
I saw that Death's unerring dart must pierce
    the friend *most* dear;
I saw the coffin, and the shroud, the poor
    corse pale and wan,
I saw the mourners weeping o'er their hopes
    forever gone;

I felt a cold hand on my heart, a sad voice
   said to me,
"What God hath hidden from frail man, he
   should not ask to see."

The vision passed, I awoke, the sun poured
   forth his light,   .
But his bright rays could not dispel the vision of that night—
My friends live on, but every day I feel a
   chilly fear
That e'er another's sun is set their home will
   not be here.
Oh! never again will I wish to peer into forbidden things,
Sufficient unto every day is the good or ill
   it brings.

MYSTERY.

BY E. LOUISE MILLS.

I HEARD a singer at early dawn,
While soft winds sighed o'er the verdant
    lawn,
Warble a sweet and silvery lay,
And this was the song that woke the day—
Mystery, mystery every-where,
In the earth and in the air,
In praises wide in the hills, and vales,
And its voice is in the whispering gales;
In dew-drop that falls from summer Heaven,
In the frost that gems the winter even,
In the little moth with silver wings.
Mystery, mystery here and there,
In land and sea, on earth, in air.
Then she laid her down by a streamlet's side,
Listened and laughed as she watched it glide;
She said, "some spirits are floating along,
I feel their breath, I hear their song."
Then she saw a bird with crimson crest
Pause on his flight to bathe his breast,

And he poured forth such a strain of song
She thrilled with joy as he warbled on.   .
Then thought she of God, who thus peopled
    the air,
And she sang on, there's mystery every-
    where;
To the ocean she went, and heard it roar
As it rushed from its caves and bathed the
    shore;
She stood and shuddered with chilly fear,
As she thought how cold the watery bier;
Well she knew there were pearls deep in its
    bed,
Then she thought of the coral towers so
    red
Reared up like monuments o'er the dead;
Then thought of the whale that sported
    there,
Of the little nautilus, slight and fair,
And she still sang, there's mystery every
    where;
Then she knelt on the beach and breathed a
    prayer
To the God of sea, and earth, and air,

Who made the ocean, wild and blue,
And formed the tiniest florets too;
Oh! let my spirit be stayed on thee,
Thou God of love and mystery.

www.ingramcontent.com/pod-product-compliance
Lightning Source LLC
Chambersburg PA
CBHW032314280326
41932CB00009B/804